# THE UNSTOPPABLE TEAM

*A simple formula for managing your team, reducing overwhelm, and increasing revenue*

Lia Garvin

THE UNSTOPPABLE TEAM

*A simple formula for managing your team, reducing overwhelm, and increasing revenue*

LIA GARVIN

Copyright © 2024 – Reflek Publishing

All Rights Reserved.

No part of this publication may be reproduced, distributed, or transmitted in any form or by any means, including photocopying, recording, or other electronic or mechanical methods, without the prior written permission of the publisher, except in the case of brief quotations embodied in critical reviews and certain other noncommercial uses permitted by copyright law.

Disclaimer: The author makes no guarantees concerning the level of success you may experience by following the advice and strategies contained in this book, and you accept the risk that results will differ for each individual. The purpose of this book is to educate, entertain, and inspire.

For more information: hello@liagarvin.com

ISBN PAPERBACK: 978-1-962280-12-9
ISBN EBOOK: 978-1-962280-13-6

# Here's a gift before you dive in!

Thank you for purchasing *The Unstoppable Team* and trusting me as your guide to making managing and running your team easier—because, spoiler, if you're a business owner with a team, you *are* a manager!

As a result of reading this book and implementing the strategies and tools I talk about, your team will not only be more motivated and higher performing, managing your team will feel more effortless and less overwhelming for you, even during crunch times.

To get you some immediate support before we even get started, head to **liagarvin.com/unstoppable** to grab your freebies and bonuses.

Resources include:

- Exclusive discounts on my services (yep, they're *only* for folks who have picked up a copy of this book)
- Thriving Team Scorecard with ten things you can do *this* week to be a better manager for your team
- Ops Playbook Savings Calculator to learn how much money you're leaving on the table by *not* implementing the strategies we'll talk about in the book (get ready for your mind to be blown)
- Link to schedule your *free* Scale-Up Strategy Call to figure out a game plan for getting support for your team
- Link to schedule a Team Whisperer SOS Call to get solutions to solve a specific challenge you are stuck in
- And more . . .

liagarvin.com/unstoppable

This book is dedicated to
my daughter, Maya,
my inspiration for making
the workplace a better place
for everyone.

# Table of Contents

Introduction .................................................................................. 9
Chapter 1: You Are a Visionary ............................................... 19
Chapter 2: Start with Your Priorities ...................................... 27
Chapter 3: Onboarding for Success ........................................ 41
Chapter 4: Expectations Are the Recipe for Scale ................ 57
Make a Lasting Impact in Real Time ..................................... 75
Chapter 5: Work Tracking ....................................................... 77
Chapter 6: Delegating and Decisions ..................................... 97
Chapter 7: Evaluating Performance ...................................... 111
Chapter 8: Make It Simple and Scalable .............................. 127
Next Steps ............................................................................... 131
Acknowledgments .................................................................. 133
Author Bio .............................................................................. 135

The tools and strategies didn't require more work on the business owner's end or make them feel like they had gotten everything wrong and needed to start over; they were simple shifts that together made a huge impact. The business started being more profitable, the teams were happier, and the business owners finally had time back for themselves.

# Introduction

When you envisioned starting your business, what did you picture?

The freedom of being your own boss? The ability to bring the idea burning inside you out into the world? Getting more time to spend with your friends and family? Maybe trips around the world on a private jet because your business is so successful?

Whatever it was for you, we all imagined something.

And as we started getting into the details of running our businesses and finding customers and serving our customers and hiring employees and making tough decisions and firing employees and figuring out when to give raises and everything in between, we might have found that all of this team stuff was *way* harder than we thought it would be. In fact, managing a team is one of the *hardest* things about running a business.

When you're juggling all the balls, making all the decisions, thinking about your business around the clock, unsure where money is being spent, unclear on what the status of work is, not ready to make a hire that you really, *really* need to make, worrying that you are the only person focused on growing your business, wondering if employees like working in your company and plan to stay—even some flavor of these—a new dream comes into the picture.

Wouldn't it feel like a dream to know people are working on the right things? To see at a glance the status of projects? To know exactly what someone will be working on when they join your team? To rest assured that employees are working at the same standard as you? To know what *you* should be focusing your time on?

The good news is that none of these things have to feel like a dream.

This book is the simple answer to these questions. It is about to make all the messy stuff that keeps you awake at night and prevents you from being able to step more than two inches away from your phone while on vacation a whole lot easier.

After reading it, you'll no longer feel like you have to figure it all out alone because you don't have to. I'm now right here with you, cheering you on, rooting for your business, giving you all the tools I have learned over the years and shared with countless business owners like you, which have saved them time, money, and most of all, stress.

This book is for you if you want to feel ease and flow in managing your team, including the following:

- Transforming your team members into profit-generating machines
- Having employees hit the ground running and make an impact from day one

## Introduction

- Creating consistency in what your clients experience from your business and team, especially as you scale your footprint
- Recouping time every single week to focus on what *you* want to focus on and let go of all the rest
- Understanding the status of work happening on your team, people's capacity, and when is the right time to hire someone new
- Seeing maximum results and output from your team members without burning people out
- And saving an average of thirty hours across your business, every single month

Having a handle on your team operations makes the difference between having a business that thrives and one that fails, and this book is your roadmap to not only having a handle on it but to putting simple, lightweight structures in place that allow you to sustain it.

In this book, we will cover my simple yet comprehensive formula for streamlining your team operations. Born from my decade of experience driving team operations in some of the most influential companies in tech, seeing the differences between teams that could rise to the occasion and deliver great results against all odds and those that couldn't deliver even with all the resources in the world, my Ops Playbook system is your window into how to scale while reducing stress and overwhelm.

*The Unstoppable Team* dives into the six focus areas of my Ops Playbook system—these are the areas where I saw the biggest breakdowns in communication happen on teams within small and large companies, and encompass the areas teams need the most clarity to do their best work.

In this book, we will talk about the following:

- **Priorities** – Often clear in the business owner's mind, a lack of understanding of priorities and what's most important is typically one of the biggest disconnects on a team. By making priorities concrete and tangible and showing how every role fits into the bigger picture, we create a team where every single person is working to grow the business.
- **Onboarding** – We work tirelessly to bring in the right employees into our team and yet often miss the critical step of creating an effective onboarding process. Onboarding sets the tone for your team member's relationship with your business, and getting it right ensures that the person hits the ground running to work effectively and stay on the team long-term.
- **Expectations** – If you want to see it happening, you've got to spell it out. Setting clear expectations is your key to not only *seeing* the behaviors you want exhibited on your team but also saving countless hours of miscommunications and disconnects because people weren't on the same page.
- **Work tracking** – A system composed of Post-Its, notes apps, and spreadsheets, all with varying levels of detail is a recipe for confusion, project delays, and overwhelm. A system used consistently (whatever it is) with a well-defined level of detail will allow you to scale and always have a window into the bandwidth of your employees and the status of active projects.

Introduction

- **Delegating and decisions** – The buck doesn't need to stop with you . . . for everything. Employees having autonomy over the micro-decisions surrounding their roles fuels their sense of accountability, and figuring out which decisions you do and do not need to make is your key to getting there.
- **Performance** – Success can't feel like a moving goalpost, no matter if you're the second-in-command in the company or working as a vendor on a project for two days. We all need to know what success looks like and the criteria used to measure it so we're motivated to do a good job and improve our performance over time.

While you can certainly dive back into chapters after you've read them, I encourage you to read the book in order the first time to get a full sense of all of the pieces and how everything fits together. For example, performance measurement is arbitrary without clear priorities and expectations. This book is written intentionally to be a quick read, to not make you wade through templates and documents and frameworks to know what to do next. I want you to get the tools, hopefully see yourself in the stories I share, and be on your way to managing your team successfully.

At first glance, the six focus areas might feel overwhelming—as in, "I have to deal with *all six* of these things?" But I assure you, it's simpler than you think. That's exactly why I do the work that I do.

Growing up in the corporate world, getting work done on teams always felt so cumbersome. Budgets had multi-layered approval processes, planning and goal-setting activities required infinite reviews and iterations, two people would be working on the same thing and not even realize it, one meeting could throw off the priorities for a whole quarter, few were clear on how to weigh tradeoffs and re-prioritize or what shifts in priorities were even based on. All of these issues created continual thrash and stress for both the team members and the managers. I looked around and thought to myself, "Does this all really have to be so complicated?"

To me, the answer was no. Time and again, when I'd make simple shifts on the teams I supported to open up communication, clarify expectations, align around roles and responsibilities, ensure everyone had the information they needed to be successful, and understand what was in it for them in order to buy into a process, change would happen overnight.

The complicated immediately became simple.

A deep focus on teams and unlocking everything we can to make it easier to get work done is and has always been my passion. Like, 'spend-my-free-time-reading-books-about-organizational-effectiveness-and-how-to-build-great-teams' passion. I love helping people find ways to work better together, to get to the outcomes they're trying to achieve more easily, to use their mental energy on solving hard problems instead of being frustrated by how hard it is to get things done.

There were many times in my career when I got feedback that I was focusing on the wrong things, that I should focus on the "work stuff first and people stuff later," or that the work I did belonged in HR. But this work *is* and always has been about the "work stuff."

## Introduction

Unsticking the places that are slowing people down or creating confusion to help people get their work done faster and with more ease yields better results. The employees win, the customers win, and the businesses win.

When I left after a decade in the big tech where I drove team operations at Microsoft, Apple, and Google to launch my consulting business, my initial plan was to focus on supporting teams in the corporate world. Some of the big challenges I saw teams wrestle with every day included unskilled managers, challenges with giving and receiving feedback, and fear around change and uncertainty; and I was eager to make these kinds of abstract and sometimes intangible topics more actionable and engaging.

While I love developing and facilitating workshops, the model of teaching one to many has the power to plant a lot of seeds but not always transform the way the businesses are working. It felt like I could make an even bigger impact.

As a new entrepreneur and business owner, when I started to connect with more and more business owners like you, it hit me like a ton of bricks that the opportunity to really drive transformation was with *you*.

Business owners like you told me time and again, "*We* are the ones who need these tools you're talking about—help us!" And when I began to share my strategies and tools with business owners, their companies started to change for the better. The tools and strategies didn't require more work on the business owner's end or make them feel like they had gotten everything wrong and needed to start over;

they were simple shifts that together made a huge impact. The business started being more profitable, the teams were happier, and the business owners finally had time back for themselves.

All of the pain points I'm talking about might feel really overwhelming and complicated right now, and I feel you because as a business owner, I'm in the thick of it too. And trust me when I say that I'm here to show you the path of how to make things easier for your team, and equally important, for yourself.

The beauty of being a business owner or entrepreneur is that you don't have all of the red tape a corporation might have to make what should be simple changes. You can launch a new task-tracking tool if the existing process isn't working, you can reframe how you evaluate performance, and you can delegate more. It's all in your control. The possibilities of what you can achieve truly are endless.

Managing a team is not something we just wake up one morning and know how to do. It's complicated and messy, and everyone brings their own style of communicating. Things can feel great one day and like a total disaster the next. We all have our superpowers and gifts. As the Team Whisperer, mine is to quickly sus out what is and is not working on a team and gain the buy-in from the team needed to implement the changes that will make things better. I am the translator between leaders and their teams so we can put the vision into action.

The strategies I talk about in this book are about making your life easier *and* making it easier for your teams to work in your company. As a result, you will see higher retention, happier employees, and a better quality of work.

*Introduction*

Thank you for trusting me to be your guide on this journey to figure out how to build your best possible team and grow your business to heights you never thought possible. I am so excited to see where you go from here.

The *how* is the circulatory system pumping blood through all of your ideas, dreams, and goals. It is the implementation, the plan, and the roadmap for translating the vision into action.

# Chapter 1
# You Are a Visionary

"I feel like every time I talk to my employees, they ask me when they're getting a raise. It's exhausting." It was so clear what the issue was, and yet, so hard to see when you're in the thick of it.

This business owner, Lisa, was frustrated, and I didn't blame her. Literally, every time she had a meeting with one of her employees, they were asking to get paid more. And let's just say this employee wasn't knocking it out of the park with their work.

I asked her, "Have you had a conversation with your team about when raises and bonuses happen?"

"No," she said, "we just kind of do them when it feels right."

"Totally get it—but if your team member is asking you for a raise, that means they've been mustering up the courage to ask you about it for a *while*. And if they're asking you more and more frequently, my guess is they're also probably looking for a new job."

The answer was simple.

From the macro level: communication. But from a more tactical standpoint: clarity.

Share with your team members what happens when, essentially *how* work gets done on your team so they *don't* have to ask you every seventeen minutes.

The *how* includes all of the things that make your business function and propel work forward. It's all the stuff we will talk about in this book. Priorities tell people *how* to focus their time, onboarding shows people *how* to get up to speed in their roles, expectations show people *how* to be successful, work tracking shows everyone *how* to ascertain the status of active work, delegating decisions shows people *how* to be accountable, performance shows people *how* they are doing relative to the expectations.

Reflecting on this, you might be thinking, "Gosh, shouldn't I have all of this figured out already?"

I'm guessing you're somewhere on the spectrum of not having realized you should have at least *thought* about some of this before—and completely beating yourself up for not having mastered everything already. Wherever you are on this continuum is perfectly fine. You're invited to the party.

As a business owner, you are the visionary. You had a dream, you saw a need, you recognized an opportunity—and you made it happen. You invested time, energy, and money into bringing this vision to life. As part of this, you're also clear on what you are going to deliver, what makes what you're doing unique, and why whatever you do is better than how anyone else would do it. You own the *why* and the *what*.

## Chapter 1

The *why* and the *what* will get you customers, they will attract talent, they will entice investors and seed money, they will bring in speaking gigs, and they will get you Instagram followers. And I'm guessing you've reaped many of these benefits already.

But there is a third piece of the equation, which is, I'll say again, the difference between businesses that thrive and those that fail: the *how*. The *how* is the circulatory system pumping blood through all of your ideas, dreams, and goals. It is the implementation, the plan, and the roadmap for translating the vision into action.

Teams don't just figure out the how on their own. We all bring our own unique ways of working, relationships with time, socializations, experiences, and perspectives—all things that make teams great and at the same time make it tough to get everyone on the same page.

Business owners don't just figure out the how on their own either, simply because they know the why and the what.

The *how* is a different beast. It takes a different level of thinking, one that's much more "boots on the ground" than you might be used to or comfortable with. As the visionary, you're all about the bigger picture and getting people bought into that picture. The little logistical or implementation details don't necessarily faze you—or they stress you the hell out, but you don't know how to tackle them.

The good news is there are actually people who *enjoy* figuring out all of the little details, who look at a vision and immediately think of a list of ideas and insights about what will need to happen to bring that vision to life.

And I'm one of those people. :)

Consider this your spell book to figure out this missing third piece that has been weighing down your business and causing you overwhelm, and consider me the person who can get you from where you are today to where you want to be in six to twelve months.

If at any point you want some hands-on support, reach out to me at **hello@liagarvin.com** or head to **liagarvin.com/unstoppable** to schedule a free Scale-Up Strategy Call to get some actionable tips specific to your business to try right away (along with the freebies and bonuses that come along with this book). Sometimes when we start to look behind the curtain, there's a little more stuff piled up than we realized. That's okay, it's to be expected.

Don't be afraid of the mess—but don't add to the mess by avoiding it either.

As the quote by Maya Angelou says, "Do the best you can until you know better. Then, when you know better, do better."

You don't have to figure out the how on your own. And you're not wrong or bad at what you do because you don't already have it figured out or you're in the midst of trying to figure it out and it isn't going so great. It's okay if a lot of the stuff I talk about in this book hasn't occurred to you. That is what I'm here for: to help you do better for your team, for your business, and for yourself.

One of the most exciting parts of my work is sitting down with a business owner like you, and while running through diagnostic questions similar to what I will share in each chapter, I see their eyes light up the moment they realize they actually have a way better handle on this team stuff than they thought they did. The answers are inside you—but they're hard to extract when you're in the thick of it.

My vision for you is that as you read this book and implement the strategies I talk about, and beyond saving the average of thirty hours a month that businesses that I support in implementing this system benefit from, you get closer to that sense of freedom that you longed for when you created the business.

After working with Rebecca Cafiero, CEO of The Pitch Club, and launching the Ops Playbook across her team, she shared, "In just a little over forty days, we should be completely profitable with an area of business that was only costing money, which is not only great for the bottom line, but it's just great from an energetic standpoint for me because I don't feel such pressure to always be the one that has to create the clients and the sales."

You don't have to be burdened with the weight of growing your business on your shoulders alone. But you can't just keep doing the same thing or ignoring the little problems that start adding up over time, hoping they'll work themselves out.

The team member complaining they are overwhelmed and overworked even though you're pretty sure the work they are doing isn't even growing the business—that person starts to be the cause of other team members feeling frustrated, unsupported, and unengaged in their work.

The team member you brought in quickly because you were desperate for someone to fill an immediate need, that you hoped would figure things out but is still kind of floundering—that person leaves within three months, resulting in having to start the hiring process all over again.

Those things like email signatures and meeting agendas and work hours that you know you've asked for a *million times* and are avoiding giving feedback on because you don't want to come across as a micromanager—those keep tripping up productivity and fuel a growing sense of resentment of your team members.

The timesheet with the overtime hours that you have a hunch shouldn't be billed but you don't feel like you have a good enough sense of that employee's work to say something about—that keeps costing you hundreds if not thousands of dollars a month.

Those little decisions that you know you should let go of because *they don't even matter,* but you literally don't have five free minutes to hand them off to a team member—those show your team members you don't trust them to make trivial decisions about their own jobs.

The awkwardness in the performance review conversation when your employee thought they were crushing it but you have to deliver feedback you've been sitting on that they didn't meet the mark—that degrades trust in your team, resulting in many meetings to get back on the same page at best, and at worst, the team member quitting.

I don't share these examples to scare you. I share them to remind you that the things that feel small and insignificant in one moment can build up over time and have a catastrophic impact on your team.

But the exciting thing is that if they weren't so catastrophic, then fixing them wouldn't be so transformational.

As Rashae Doyle, CEO of BevelUp, shared about her experience with the Ops Playbook system, "It has taken the burden of being an 'issues manager' or 'guidance counselor' for the team off my shoulders and given them the freedom to move through challenges with confidence. The team now has a resource that clearly defines how success looks at BevelUp and it has given me the freedom to focus on building the brand."

This is where the fun starts. This is where you get to put on your X-ray glasses to finally understand the breakdowns in communication and efficiencies happening on your team, getting in the way of seamless flow in your business.

Ready to do this?

Buckle up.

When we shared the top priority back with the team, that it was part of everyone's jobs to hit this revenue target, and gave clear examples of what that meant for each role, the team got it. They were excited to take a more active role in growing the business, they just hadn't known that was the expectation before.

## Chapter 2
# Start with Your Priorities

"We need help narrowing down the P0s for this quarter," the product manager said nervously to the VP of engineering. "There are thirty-seven P0s, but we only have five people on the team to do all the work."

"I can't narrow anything down," the VP replied. "Every single item on this list is important and has to get done this quarter. End of story."

"Okay . . . will do," replied the product manager, his face very much reading, *Will not do,* but what else was there to say? This was a team in which you just say yes, even if it was impossible, knowing full well you'll have to explain later why something didn't get done that was *never* going to get done in the first place.

It was a team where people worked around the clock, always feeling like they were coming up short when it got to the end of the quarter and projects didn't get finished. People felt tense in meetings, afraid that any idea shared would result in even more work to take on. They weren't sure what to work on first, since everything is deemed as *most* important, so they just picked something off the list and chipped away at it, leaving a series of half-finished projects and no sense of completion. And after the performance review season, when people got credit for sprinting the marathon and collected their bonuses, people left the team.

Let's just say, it wasn't a good situation.

*P0* is the term in the tech world for "most, most, most important thing, like, *nothing else happens* until this thing gets done," and yet, in every single job I've ever had, the scenario unfolds just as it did in that quarterly planning meeting. We have too many priorities. Everything feels important. Hell, everything *is* important. But just because we believe it's important and really, really want it to get done, it doesn't mean it will. And when we set our teams up for failure by strong-arming them into agreeing to work they know will not get done, we've created a pattern where people don't have to be accountable for what they agree to.

It can be equally difficult to be accountable for vague priorities.

A priority means the one most important thing—emphasis on *thing*. I was on a team years ago where the priority was to "save a billion lives." This was a compelling vision statement, but it fell short as a priority for the team because we had no idea what work we were supposed to do in support of that. What was the task list for saving a billion lives? How would one break that up into a quarter-by-quarter or even an annual plan? The broadness of the priority made it feel impossible, and again, just like in the *too many priorities* situation, team members lost faith in the leader because they didn't understand what they were working toward.

Our teams don't want to let us down. They want to say "yes." Alright fine, we all have those team members who say "no" to even the simplest things, but for the sake of argument, let's say on the whole we've hired great people and they want to do great work.

When we have thirty-seven P0s (or priorities that are really vision statements), we put our teams in the tough spot where they know they're not set up for success but don't know what to do about it. Then when priorities inevitably *don't* get accomplished, we're all disappointed and frustrated. As the business owner or team leader, you're mad because people said they could get it done and you believed them. And your team is mad because you didn't listen when they tried to push back. Lose-lose.

Before I get to the good stuff of how to fix this, I want to dive a little deeper into the cost of having unclear priorities.

Priorities serve as your north star, the thing you are all collectively working toward. When half of your team thinks one thing is important and the other half thinks something else is important, and neither of those is what *you* think is most important, you have exactly zero people on the team working on what's most important.

You also lose a sense of ownership, and this is a concept I'll talk a lot about because it's the game-changing mindset that will give you a competitive edge and set your business up to grow and scale. Our team members feel a sense of ownership when they understand the plan and can see themselves in it. By contrast, they are not going to go near owning something with a ten-foot pole if it feels like there's no way to accomplish it. Priority-setting isn't an episode of *Storage Wars*;

people should understand exactly what they're buying into when they commit to it.

The results of a lack of ownership on teams are far-reaching, but the one that often immediately sticks out for the business owners I support is team members doing the bare minimum in their jobs. They complete the task, they check the box, and they do the assignment. No more, no less. They don't think beyond the task about the *best way* to solve a problem or deliver a service to a client. Why would they? No one has communicated what the bigger picture is. As a result, you're not able to unlock your team members' full creative potential, and it's hard for customers to differentiate your services from others because the work happening in your team *isn't* above and beyond.

Priorities also set what order to work on things, meaning what to work on next doesn't become an arbitrary decision a team member makes once they finish something. This again saves time and money because folks are working on the right things at all times, and projects are being worked to completion instead of being left half-finished.

## Where do we go *wrong* with setting priorities?

Too many priorities or too vague of priorities—priorities are not to-do lists or vision statements.

## So What Do We Do About It?

I worked with a PR firm whose owner felt like she was the only one in the business thinking about the importance of growing and maintaining their client base. She built her company from the ground up, and from the onset, business development and new client acquisition was her responsibility. As her team grew, she was paying people competitive salaries and offering great opportunities, but no one really saw it as their responsibility to think about the business side of things. She'd constantly be thinking about sales and client outreach during the day, at dinner with her kids, in the evening before bed, on the weekends at her son's soccer game, every minute of the day. It was on her to keep the business alive.

As we worked through the Ops Playbook system where I support businesses hands-on in mapping out and implementing the strategies shared in this book, we outlined a clear priority for her business over the next twelve months. The goal was to hit a specific revenue target, reflective of growing to a certain size to deliver value to more clients and have a company where her team members could see their career goals met.

Sidenote: To establish the priorities for your team, I recommend using the SMART Goals framework (specific, measurable, attainable, realistic, and timely) developed by George Doran, Arthur Miller, and James Cunningham.[1] This helps to avoid the "too many priorities" because you're making sure they are attainable and the "too vague of priorities" because you're making them specific and timely.

Once we had the revenue target priority for the PR firm, we then mapped out how each role in her team connected to this priority, clarifying specifics within the day-to-day of their job. And when

---

1. George T. Doran, "There's a S.M.A.R.T. Way to Write Management's Goals and Objectives," *Management Review 70* (1981): 35–36.

I say specific, I mean *real* specific. For example, for the PR account manager: "One month before the end of the engagement, start talking about ideas you have for keeping the momentum going in the clients' campaign."

When we shared the top priority back with the team, that it was part of *everyone's jobs* to hit this revenue target, and gave clear examples of what that meant for each role, the team got it. They were excited to take a more active role in growing the business; they just hadn't known that was the expectation before.

With a clear priority and line of sight into the kinds of activities that would support it, they could then bring additional creative ideas to the table for how to get there. And they blew it out of the water. Within weeks, two of the account managers brought in $13,000 of new business, all because they now *knew* that contributing to the revenue goal was a required part of their job and would be factored into how they were going to be evaluated.

And for that business owner, she was able to finally take a vacation and actually turn off her work emails and chats, soak up the sun with her husband and kids, and genuinely enjoy herself, knowing that she now had her whole team invested in and accountable to growing the business. She had created a team of owners.

## Where do we go *right* with setting priorities?

Use the SMART goals framework and connecting the dots. Employees need to see where our company is going and how they fit into the picture.

## It's Our Job to Connect the Dots

Priorities aren't just for building alignment; when done right, they reduce overwhelm because our team members aren't confused about what is most important. This is why it's so critical to not have too many priorities because then it is just a to-do list.

People want to feel like they are part of something bigger than themselves. Having clear priorities helps fuel a stronger sense of purpose in our work because we see how we fit into the bigger picture. When you have a team where everyone does very different kinds of work, priorities serve as the connective tissue across each of the roles, because at the end of the day, everyone is working toward the same goal.

For the PR firm CEO in the example from earlier in this chapter, setting a clear priority around revenue allowed her to rally everyone around a shared goal. Team members shifted their mindsets from being focused on individual tasks to how their work laddered up to that bigger goal. We could then set clear performance targets around the revenue priority because everyone knew the specific actions they needed to take to get there (e.g., in their case, supporting the extension of PR coverage for existing clients).

For businesses with employees who have more tactical roles (e.g., cleaning equipment in a MedSpa or gym, answering phones, fulfilling shipping orders), understanding the company priorities and where they fit into the picture is transformational in moving team members from feeling like a cog in a machine to someone whose job is indispensable. It is our job as the business owner and team leader to connect the dots for our team members and show them why their job matters, no matter what it is.

I learned this lesson a few years ago when I was managing a team of program managers (essentially project managers who oversee several related projects that together compose a "program") at Google. In a one-on-one meeting with one of my direct reports, she said in passing that her role was to be a "professional nag" and expressed frustration because she didn't see how that could amount to a fulfilling career.

I stopped in my tracks when I heard this—not only was this perspective negatively impacting how she approached her work and limiting the options she saw for her career as a whole, it was also a total misrepresentation of the value of the role.

"I gotta stop you right there," I said, "and it's not just because I spent a decade working as a program manager and think that's the worst possible way to talk about the work. Do you want to know how *I* see this role and your role on our team? You are a strategic partner to your design, engineering, and product partners—the connective tissue across the departments, understanding the bigger picture, foreseeing risks, and charting the course for how to get an incredibly complex project with competing priorities and demands done on time. How in the world is that a 'professional nag'?"

Her eyes lit up as I explained this. "I never thought of it that way."

"Apparently not," I joked. "When you think of the role as nagging or babysitting work, that's how you're going to approach it, and then it's going to be a self-fulfilling prophecy. What would it look like to approach it from this strategic lens?"

By putting out this question, she was able to see where the "professional nag" label was impacting her work. For example, instead of emailing people "Is this done yet," or "Me again," she'd proactively communicate expectations and hold people accountable to the deadlines that were agreed on. Putting on the strategic hat allowed her to reframe how she communicated with people from chasing down details to setting up the system for people to understand what to get done. No more nagging needed.

Paint the picture for all of your team members of why their work matters and how it serves in accomplishing the priorities of the business and you will see them rise to the occasion. I'm gonna go Don Draper for a minute and give examples of how to do this. Hear me out because it isn't blowing smoke; it helps create a stronger sense of meaning.

The person responsible for keeping the equipment clean at your gym or MedSpa?

*At this business, we want to create a premium experience for our clients and customers, somewhere where everything feels effortlessly taken care of. That means when they walk through the door, all equipment is in impeccable shape and ready to use, meticulously taken care of by the cleaning tech. As a result, clients come back regularly and recommend us to their friends and network, our business grows, and we hit our revenue and profit targets.*

The team member in charge of packing and shipping out the orders?

*We know our customers have no shortage of choice in who they buy from these days, and with Amazon literally promising to drone ship packages in two hours, we have to make it worthwhile to buy from us. The packing/fulfilling role is the key to this. Carefully wrapping and packing items, writing a handwritten note, and shipping them out immediately ensures our customers see that they are buying from a retailer that cares about them and their experience; and in turn, they continue to shop with us, recommend us to their friends, and share their experience on social media.*

Your team members are looking to you to paint the vision for them, and when you do it effectively so they can really see themselves in it, they will show up differently. I know it because I saw it with my program manager who never again saw herself as a professional nag, and I know it because it has worked with every small business I've supported with the Ops Playbook system. And I mean, it just makes sense, right? Why would you care about growing a business that doesn't care about *you?*

## Diagnostic Questions

When thinking about your team priorities, consider the following questions:

- What is your big company goal for the next six to twelve months? What metric can you tie to it (revenue, number of clients served, number of locations, etc.)?
- How do you determine the most important thing to work on?
- What is the work associated with that big priority for *every* role or department in your company?
- If priorities change, how is it communicated to your team?

## Priorities Support the Vision, Mission, and Values

We already talked about the fact that priorities are not vision statements, but that doesn't mean you don't *need* a vision statement. A vision, mission, and supporting team values are critical to developing and communicating with your team in order to have everyone aligned around the bigger picture. Priorities are the things that are the most important to do first for a given period of time, to work toward that vision. A vision is something that likely won't be completed in our lifetimes, or certainly not in the immediate future; priorities are typically set for a quarter, six-month, or annual time frame.

When working with clients on determining their priorities using the SMART goals framework I mentioned, we start by talking about the vision, mission, and values. Otherwise, what the hell are the priorities based on?

Values are the beliefs or behaviors that we embody as a company. While there's a lot of debate out there about whether company/team values should be aspirational or reflective of how you are showing up today (and the book *The Advantage* by Patrick Lencioni talks about different lenses for values and how to come up with them for your team), you will want to align with values that feel authentic to you. Tactically, I like to pair values with a clarifying statement explaining what they mean, because individual words can be abstract and mean something totally different to everyone. For example: *Authenticity—we show up the same with our clients as we do with each other and ensure clients feel like they are getting the same person when they work with us in person as they see online.*

Your values will govern how you make decisions, what kinds of clients you serve, and you guessed it, what your priorities are ;) especially in terms of the kind of work that supports achieving them. Values that really prioritize a service-minded way of operating—which, let's face it, we all should have if we want our clients to love us—will have priorities and supporting responsibilities that help us better serve our clients.

To clear up one more thing before we wrap, it's okay to have revenue-based goals. Our goals don't have to be about saving the world to be worthy or honorable. High revenues and profits allow us to serve more clients, deliver better results, and provide more jobs and career opportunities for people. We just want to be mindful of framing them in the context of how that revenue goal benefits our clients and employees—i.e., it's not about your team burning the midnight oil so you can get rich. And I know you don't think that, but you still have to spell it out so there's no room for error.

**It's Not Too Late!**

If you're reading this worried you've done everything wrong and it's too late for you and your business, re-read this section heading: it's not too late. In fact, it's not too late for any of the stuff we'll talk about in this book.

Regarding team priorities and connecting the dots between work and priorities, you can call a meeting at *any* time (or bring it as an agenda item to an existing team meeting), where the goal is to bring more clarity across the team on what the priorities are and how each role fits into the bigger picture. Depending on the size of the company, you could meet with everyone one-on-one to talk through it.

I like the following framing, and feel free to literally pull this directly:

"Hey, everyone, I was thinking about where we are going with this business and am so excited about what the future holds. And then it hit me that I might not have done enough to bring all of you along into where we are going and how each of your roles fits into the bigger picture." Boom, proceed.

This frames the conversation as an opportunity, not something missing or that people did wrong; and it also implies their roles should have always been aligned with the company priorities, you're just making it more clear now. Open the door for team members to ask questions and share anywhere they need further clarification, especially if they're not seeing how their specific role fits into the bigger picture. This kind of conversation builds trust with team members, ensures they're on the same page as to what is most important, and shows them you are investing in their success.

**Let's Recap**

- Priorities establish what is most important to focus on over a certain period of time.
- When setting priorities, we want to avoid having too many priorities or too vague of priorities.
- We create a sense of ownership and accountability to the priorities of our businesses and a team where everyone is collectively working to grow the business when we connect the dots between every role and the company priorities.

With clear priorities set and a sense of ownership across our teams, we're ready to make sure every new team member is set up for success as they join your business or change roles within your business.

Let's dive into onboarding.

The most excited our employees will ever be is on that first day.
And having an effective onboarding process is our opportunity to harness and fuel that excitement to last for months and months.

# Chapter 3
# Onboarding for Success

It was my first day of work at my new job, and I pulled into the underground parking lot of the high-rise beaming with excitement. This was going to be the day when my career took on the trajectory it was always supposed to.

I parked the car, turned down the '90s dance jams that are always my music of choice to get pumped up (I mean, how can you listen to "La Bouche" and *not* get hyped?), and took a few deep breaths. I was greeted in the lobby by a warm and friendly executive assistant who welcomed me to the team and escorted me to the elevator and our floor to find my office. *I have an office?!* I thought. *Yeah, this is going to be amazing.*

Moving from San Francisco to Seattle wasn't an easy decision, but it felt like one I had no choice but to make. I was recruited to join a tech company, something I had wanted to do for as long as I could remember having grown up in the San Francisco Bay Area, and the company even paid for me to relocate. The catch was I had just gotten married and my husband was in school, so I'd have to move to a new city by myself and navigate a long-distance relationship while learning the ropes of a new job. *Worth it*, I figured. This would create more opportunities to come.

We got to my office and the executive assistant said, "Here's your office, go ahead and get settled in. Jen is at an offsite today and tomorrow, so she won't be around. Let me know if you need anything."

And then, I proceeded to spend the next eight hours sitting alone in the office, no computer, no instructions from my new manager Jen, no information, nothing. Just me and my life choices, my thoughts creeping in asking me, "*This* is what you uprooted your life for?"

The drive home that day was terrible. I wanted to be excited about the company and the job, but *really?* My manager hadn't prepared *anything* to give me *any* sense of how to get up to speed about what I would be working on or what the team was about. And she was also going to be gone the next day too?

My husband called as I was debating what to say. "How was it?!"

I burst into tears. "I don't even know. No one came in to talk to me the whole day. I sat there all day, and my manager wasn't there. She's not there again tomorrow. I think this was a mistake."

How did this job go from something I was so excited about to something that felt like a mistake?

The absence of an onboarding process.

We're all busy, I get it. And often when we've hired someone, it's because we were so freakin' busy with all of the work we had to do that the *last thing* on our minds is ramping up the new person in their new role. But I also know firsthand the second-guessing that happens on the employee's side when you join a team and get no support.

The most excited our employees will *ever be* is on that first day. And having an effective onboarding process is our opportunity to harness and fuel that excitement to last for months upon months. It can even re-energize and uplift the spirits of other team members who have been in your company for a while. Or we can instantly extinguish that flame by forgetting about onboarding.

The Society for Human Resource Management, the world's largest HR association with over 325K members, reports that 90% of new hires decide if they're going to be at a company for the long haul within their first six months,[2] and I'd argue that decision is influenced by the first few days—especially if it's a bad experience. It's hard to shake that. And let's be real (and to overgeneralize), with younger Millennials and GenZ being known to have little tolerance for sticking around in work situations they don't like, I think there are a lot of folks in my situation who wouldn't have come back for day two. Just sayin'.

While having zero onboarding process is an extreme case, a much more common scenario is having a minimal process that doesn't give a new team member a sense of where to find information, what to focus on for the first few weeks, or what success looks like in their role. And

---

2. Roy Maurer, "Onboarding Key to Retaining, Engaging Talent," Society for HR Management, shrm.org, April 16, 2015, https://www.shrm.org/resourcesandtools/hr-topics/talent-acquisition/pages/onboarding-key-retaining-engaging-talent.aspx#:~:text=Remember%2C%20nearly%2090%20percent%20of,sincerely%20care%2C%20he%20said.&text=Only%202%20percent%20of%20companies,according%20to%20the%20Aberdeen%20Group.

that's just as costly from a productivity standpoint and demoralizing for your new employee.

I was once mentoring an engineer at Google who had joined her team fresh out of college. Getting a job at Google was a dream come true, and as the youngest person on the team and the only woman, she was terrified of coming across like she didn't know what she was doing. Her manager gave her a starter project to work on, but there were so many nuances about the engineering process specific to Google that she kept getting stuck.

Worried people would think they made a mistake in hiring her, she tried to figure everything out by herself, spending every evening pouring through documentation and internal company web pages to make progress on her work. She came to me exhausted because she knew she was spinning her wheels on the wrong things but didn't feel comfortable asking for help.

"What was the onboarding process for this role?" I asked her. She shared that her manager met with her once to welcome her to the team and walk through her starter project and said to feel free to reach out if she had any questions.

"But I have *so many* questions," she said. "I can't email him every thirty seconds, so I feel like I shouldn't even bother him at all."

This wasn't a failing on this engineer's part. This was a failure on the manager for not onboarding her properly. Read the tea leaves, buddy. New hire fresh out of college, first job, massive company with very specific ways of working. This person needed an onboarding buddy to show her the ropes. There is no situation in which that person could feel successful without it.

Whatever size of the company, a new employee being paid to sit around and have no idea what to be working on (or wasting hours on end trying to figure out how to get their work done) is bad for business. At best, a few weeks of pay go out the door in a puff of smoke. But at worst, your new team member says "Eff this" and quits—leaving you to have to start that painful, time-consuming, and daunting hiring process that you just completed *again*.

The content platform BuiltIn reports that this can cost anywhere from $1,500 for hourly employees, to 1.5 times an employee's salary for technical positions.[3] And that doesn't account for all of *your time* that will have to go into hiring, which could otherwise be spent growing your business. When new employees are unhappy or perceive a company to be disorganized, it starts to poison the water hole; and the smaller your company is, the word spreads *quick*.

I say all of this to reiterate the importance of not falling into the trap of being too busy or underwater to onboard someone because it takes so much more time to fix the problem once it's there.

I also say it to offer you hope: the reason you might be seeing a revolving door of employees or wondering why people aren't meeting your expectations in their work is because of a lack of a simple and clear onboarding process.

---

3. Kate Heinz, "The True costs of Employee Turnover," BuiltIn, builtin.com, June 23, 2023, https://builtin.com/recruiting/cost-of-turnover.

## Where do we go *wrong* with onboarding?

Not doing it at all or missing major opportunities to set someone up for success, asking people to come to you with questions without helping them frame what they might even have questions about.

## So What Do We Do About It?

The best part about this is that mapping out an effective onboarding process is actually super easy.

As a wellness clinic owner and I were wrapping up the Ops Playbook program with her team, it became more and more clear: she needed to make a few key hires to get her out of the weeds and allow her to focus on scaling the business. Hiring two new team members was going to be a financial stretch for her, but she knew having someone looking inward at overseeing her team members and someone looking outward at marketing and partnership opportunities would fill a number of gaps that had been holding the business back from getting it to where she knew it could go.

Because it was a stretch and these were going to be two new roles for her business, she knew she'd have to both carefully craft the job descriptions to attract the kinds of employees that would elevate her business and be really thoughtful about their onboarding process since there weren't any existing protocols to draw from for the jobs. She encouraged both new hires to spend as much time as they could at the two clinic locations to get to know the other team members, build rapport, and assess where the biggest gaps were. She made herself available to meet multiple times per week to talk through questions, work through their ideas, and give feedback. I was also able to offer some coaching support on the manager side to set them up for success as new managers.

The most critical part of the onboarding was offering air-cover to the rest of the team, clearly stating that she was asking them to tackle the kind of work they were taking on and deputizing them to make decisions. This is a step we often skip when we hire someone to do a new kind of role or improve on a process or existing way of working, and the result is usually a lot of resistance from the rest of the team. Existing team members may assume the new person is trying to "prove themselves" without knowing all of the context or history and can act defensively or ignore the suggestions outright.

I'm not going to say we can avoid *all* resistance about changing things around by doing this, but it goes a long way to get you way closer to alignment. The wellness clinic owner told her team directly why she was so excited to have these two new team members on board, what they were responsible for, and how all of their work was in service of growing the business and making it easier to get work done (and in turn have thriving careers). Hearing this directly, the team understood the business owner was looking out for them. She could then set the expectation that she was tasking the new team members with making some key decisions and to please defer to *them* instead of double-checking everything with her. As a result, she could focus her time and energy on the business strategy and being the face of the company, and she had two A-players to offload work from her plate.

Tactically, an effective onboarding process has a number of key steps: outlining the Day 1 experience so no one has the experience I had at that first tech company, ensuring the new team member understands the expectations of them the first few weeks, checking in at regular intervals over the first ninety days, and pairing them up with a buddy to answer questions.

Jackie Koch, founder and CEO of the HR consulting firm People Principles, recommends putting check-ins on the calendar at thirty, sixty, and ninety days after the new team member starts. This allows you to set the expectation that there will be these opportunities to connect and check in on how things are going, and make sure not to forget to have the conversations because you put them on the calendar in advance. Having them set up in advance also prevents a new team member from worrying they did something wrong or are getting fired when a "90-day review" pops up on the calendar out of nowhere.

What I love about this is it establishes key moments where you can recognize wins, give feedback, and course-correct if things are off to a rocky start. Because both you and the new team member know the meetings are coming, you're both accountable to making the check-ins useful and productive.

## Where do we go *right* with onboarding?

Establish a plan for Day 1, ensuring your new hire feels welcome and knows how to learn more about their role; set check-ins at the 30/60/90-day marks to give feedback and fine-tune what is and isn't working; find the new hire a buddy to answer questions.

## Spoiler: Onboarding Isn't Just for New Employees

We tend to think of onboarding as something that only happens when someone starts in a new team or company. But *every time* someone starts in a new role, they have to learn the ropes all over again. I've talked to numerous business owners who have been frustrated when a star employee expresses interest in a different kind of role in the company, they give them that job, and then it's a total bust. I think the moments when it's a flop are due in large part to skipping re-onboarding.

If an employee moves from administrative to operations, or operations to marketing, or marketing to sales—they are doing a totally different job. Of course someone can't do it at maximum proficiency overnight. Set them up for success by re-onboarding them in a similar way you'd do with a new hire: setting clear expectations about the first few weeks, 30/60/90-day check-ins to give feedback, the works. Sure, they don't need to learn about the company, but they have to learn about how to do this *new job* effectively. They have to be set up for success.

I'll also caveat that just because someone rocked it at marketing, it doesn't mean they're going to be great at operations (or whatever role); and that's okay. For the sake of your business and your own sanity, be thoughtful about moving people to other roles within your team if they don't have previous experience in that kind of work. This can be especially hard if you have a close relationship with the person and they want to try a new experience and you don't want to let them down. But nothing will tank that relationship faster than if they flounder in the role and it compromises your company or bottom line. If someone has no experience in a specific kind of work and you really want to give them the chance, work together to map out a plan for how they're going to get training or mentorship in the new subject, and then have those 30/60/90-day check-ins to assess how it's going.

Re-onboarding is also needed when someone is promoted to additional responsibilities. Taking on the role as a manager is a *new job*, at least in respect to the managing part. Especially in situations when someone has never managed before, there needs to be some kind of training and onboarding about those new responsibilities to set them up for success.

On smaller teams, managers often take on a player/coach role where they both have a set of job responsibilities outside of management along with people-management responsibilities. For example, one of my clients is a marketing agency and many of their people managers are also account executives with a full slate of clients.

Taking on the role of a manager is a shift in how that person approaches their job; it's not just an add-on if you have time. In this player/coach model, you will likely have to load-balance some of the "player" work to someone who doesn't have the new responsibility of managing to free up time for the manager to focus on their team. Things like having one-on-one meetings and career conversations, troubleshooting issues, checking in on work, and potentially pinch-hitting when a direct report is out of the office are all things managers need to account for and that their team members are depending on.

A lot of people want to be managers because they like mentoring or helping people. That's an awesome start, but it's not the full picture of what managing is about. Managing includes giving feedback, having hard conversations, developing people professionally, and a whole myriad leadership skills that people need to learn so they can best support their teams.

If you have only a handful of managers, hiring a coach for a few months can be a helpful way to onboard them into this new aspect of their role; and if you have more than three, I'd invest in some kind of group training or manager development program to dive into the skills more deeply and show the group how they can lean on each other as a community of managers. I weave manager training into the implementation phase of the Ops Playbook program when I work with clients because it's such a critical piece of getting team operations right. And hey, even seasoned managers could always use a refresher on it.

**What If Someone Just Isn't a Fit?**

It sucks when it happens. You spend all of this time searching for the perfect hire, interviewing candidates, onboarding, figuring out the perfect starter projects, and making time to meet regularly . . . and then it becomes clear they're just not a fit.

While I'm not an HR expert (meaning I'm not the right person to ask for detailed recommendations on how to fire someone), I will say that there is a wealth of information to learn from this experience to inform how to approach making the *next hire*. Even though it's costly to have to start the hiring process again, *nothing* is more expensive than having a team member who brings everyone else down.

In this situation, don't wallow in being mad at yourself for making a bad hire. Any time we hire someone, we're taking a gamble. Someone said all of the right things in the interview and seemed so perfect. Someone had the best related experience and was going to elevate your business. Someone you knew from working in a past job together is great for a new role on the team. Until . . . they're not. Harness the moment as something you'll use as data to improve your hiring process and move forward.

Next, before you fully write the new employee off, make sure you've adequately set expectations and shared feedback on what is and isn't working. People bring all sorts of baggage into new jobs, from how they did things in their last company, to an eagerness to "make an impact" quickly that can come across as arrogant or like they're not a team player. If you want someone to spend their first few weeks in the job absorbing the culture without making recommendations, make it clear that's what you want. If you want someone to be delivering results by the end of Week 1, make that clear and set some concrete metrics or outcomes.

If it still feels like a lost cause, reflect on what about this person wasn't a fit—was it the type of job experience that really didn't mesh with what you needed, their approach to the work, their lack of listening skills? Really tune in here.

I recently spoke with a marketing CEO who hired a senior director position, choosing someone with a corporate background to bring some structure to her leadership team. But she immediately saw he rubbed people the wrong way, and employees who had been doing great work in her company for many years started coming to her frustrated. She took quick action to deliver feedback to the senior director but still felt disappointed she made the hire and was about to have to go through the whole process again.

"Think of this as a gift," I said to her. "All of the things that aren't working about this person are the things you will be more aware of and make sure to avoid as you hire the next person. Make a list of criteria of what's really important to you now that you've gone through this experience. Set clear expectations with all of your candidates about *how* you want them to approach the work. Then reiterate these expectations during the onboarding process."

She saw there was hope and that on the other side of this disappointing situation would be the senior director who really elevated her company. It just wasn't *this* guy. But armed with the reflection of what she wanted in the future, she knew it would be the next one.

## Diagnostic Questions

Along with setting up those 30/60/90-day meetings, we want to ask ourselves the following:

- What do you want the experience to be like when a new employee starts? What about even before they start?
- What are your expectations around deliverables and impact for the first few weeks?
- Where do people usually get stuck when it comes to starting in your company?

## It's Not Too Late!

Onboarded someone a few months ago and realized that you didn't do any of the things I talked about in this chapter? You guessed it, it's not too late!

Schedule a one-on-one meeting with the new hire to talk through how the first few weeks/months/however long have gone. Discuss both highlights and lowlights, where you've seen things going well or celebrating wins, and ask them where they feel like things could have been clearer or where they need support. From here, schedule another meeting thirty days out to check back in—this essentially is your new sixty-day check-in, so you have an opportunity to give feedback now that you're tuned more into the person and their work and can keep offering them support.

If it's been six months or longer, I'd still schedule this check-in meeting to see how things are going in general and ask if they need support. They are still relatively new in the grand scheme of things, and having this conversation with you might be the boost they need to keep momentum.

If you have managers on your team and haven't invested in any manager training, set down the book and find some *right now*. We all know what they say, "People don't leave companies, they leave managers." So let's make sure our businesses are the exception not the rule by giving our managers more love.

To drive retention on your team and get the best work out of your team members, always be investing in making your managers better. Join the training sessions with your managers, host a book club, or watch the video training series together to demonstrate you are also committed and accountable to showing up as a great manager. In my experience, I've found that the better managers generally opt-in to participating in trainings while the worse ones opt-out, thinking they have it *totally* dialed in and need zero additional help. At the same time, there can be a resistance on teams to having mandatory trainings.

To mitigate any resistance, model your commitment to being a great manager by actively engaging in training and development for yourself. Talk about your expectations that anyone managing people invests time in strengthening their management skills. Sharing your expectations for managers in the interviewing and onboarding phases (or re-onboarding) will also weed out folks who don't take the importance of being a great manager seriously. Even if you're really needing someone to fill a role, before tapping someone to be a manager, make sure they have a shared vision with you on the responsibility that goes into being a great manager—the cost of having ineffective managers is too high.

**Let's Recap**

- Onboarding ensures new team members feel welcome to your team, are set up for success in their work, and can make an impact right away.
- Checking in at 30/60/90-day intervals allows you to share positive and constructive feedback and course-correct where needed.
- Anytime someone is changing roles in your company (including becoming a manager on top of their existing responsibilities), onboarding is needed; it's not only for new hires. Realizing you need support for your managers? Head to **liagarvin.com/unstoppable** to setup your free Scale-up Strategy Call and I've got you covered

With a clear onboarding process getting people up to speed on your company, you can bring clarity into how to get things done.

It's time to set expectations.

Expectations are the recipe to scale, plain and simple. And I don't even mean that as a metaphor. They literally are the recipe so you can create a repeatable process or system or business model or customer experience or you-name-it across your company.

# Chapter 4
# Expectations Are the Recipe for Scale

"Why don't they just . . . ?" said every business owner ever.

It seems so obvious to us.

We say this because *we* care, *we* get it, *we* lie awake at night thinking through all of the ins and outs of our business; and when something needs to get done, *we* get right the hell on it.

As Gary Vaynerchuk points out in his content, and we know all too well, our business is *our* baby, not our employees' baby, they're never going to care about it the same way we do, and that's okay.

But they can get pretty damn close, and it comes down to setting expectations.

When we say we want someone to "just get it" or "be a second me," what we really want is to have someone read our minds and do the work as we would without having to explain everything to them. I know because, *of course*, me too.

Or maybe it's that we don't exactly know what we want. We hired a person because they seemed like an awesome self-starter with great work experience and we want them to figure it out on their own.

Again, all of this comes down to expectations.

Years ago, I was working at a branding and design agency as one of the project managers overseeing the deadlines and deliverables for our clients. When we'd kick off a new project, the studio was buzzing with excitement, every designer vying for their concept to get picked by the client. Reviews were fun and lively, and we looked forward to our meetings with the client. But as these things go, as projects progressed, the excitement started to dwindle, the biggest issue being the founder (and lead creative director) of the agency moving on to focus on business development for the next project being difficult to pin down for a review to wrap up the current projects.

One day in a meeting with the creative director, I brought up how we have a lot of energy at the start of a project but tend to lose steam by the end, and I wanted to talk with him about ideas for what to do about it.

He jumped in mid-explanation and said, "You know what we need? A process for finishing strong."

On one hand, I was a little frustrated he interrupted me to share my exact idea as if it came from *him*, but hey, it meant he was on board, so I went with it.

"Great idea," I said. "What does it mean to you to finish strong? And how can you model this for the rest of the team?"

He was stumped by the question, and this is where so many of us get stuck—knowing we want *something* different but not really knowing how to articulate it. But "I'll know it when I see it" isn't setting expectations.

Along with my work streamlining team operations, I do a lot of work coaching and training managers, and one of the biggest fears most managers have is being a micromanager. They don't want to be too far in the weeds, telling people what to do and course-correcting at every turn. In avoidance of this, they swing the pendulum too far in the other direction. They either set no expectations at all or helicopter manage, where they dip in and out of projects, creating thrash for the team.

I want to set the record straight because sometimes I think we worry that certain behaviors are micromanaging that our teams would never interpret that way. I've been managed by micromanagers, and here are some of the behaviors they displayed:

- Line editing email drafts of low-stakes communications going out to our internal team (*low stakes* meaning the email wasn't for public consumption, going to leaders in the company, or had any potentially contentious information in it).
- Continually checking in to see if I scheduled a meeting that was already on the calendar.
- Reminding me to do some obvious task that I always did and didn't need to be reminded about, like sending an agenda for a meeting or making a project plan.

The trend here is all of these little nitpicky things are happening *after* the work is already underway, sending a message that my manager didn't think I was going to handle it right. When this happens, we throw up our hands, we think "Why bother" or "Why don't they just do it themselves?"

It is expensive to be a micromanager because you are keeping one foot (maybe an arm too if your team is lucky enough) into a project that someone is already being paid to work on, distracting you from focusing on revenue-generating work or growing the business.

Micromanaging isn't something we strive to do, it's often the result of forgetting to set expectations, for communicating up front what we want to see, when we want to check in on progress, and what success looks like.

My guess is a lot of the expectations you would like to set on your team aren't micromanagey or wouldn't feel micromanagey with the right framing; and I encourage you to not let experiences with bad managers prevent you from establishing what you feel is important to see from your team.

Micromanaging is also a case of getting too specific about the way we want work to be done, implying that there's only one right way to do it (a.k.a. *your* way). By setting expectations that are more anchored to outcomes, you can leave space for your team members to meet and exceed those expectations in ways that are authentic to them.

In the case of the creative director, he wasn't micromanaging; he was setting too vague of expectations, asking for something he didn't even understand, and implying something was missing that he had never asked for.

Both of these examples prevent teams from understanding what they need to do to be successful. As a result, they make a guess and potentially waste time because they got it wrong, or you stay deep in the weeds because you haven't stopped to think about what you want upfront.

## Where do we go *wrong* with setting expectations?

Assuming the way we work is the way everyone will (or should) work, but never making it clear what that looks like.

## What Even Are Expectations?

Expectations get us on the same page as our team members and paint a picture of what success looks like for a given task, project, responsibility, or job. They are the little "agreements" we set forth with our team members about what we want to see from them. Emphasis on agreements: When we have a dynamic where we're paying someone and they've committed to upholding them, they're not hopes or wishes, they're agreements.

Most of us have had a bad experience with a manager at some point in our careers, which has left a bad taste in our mouths about managers in general. And like we just talked about, if the bad experience is due to a micromanager (which, according to a survey by staffing agency Accountemps, 59% of employees have at some point in their careers[4]), it can make us weary of setting expectations because we don't want

---

4. Accountemps, "Survey: More Than Half of Employees Have Worked for a Micromanager," PR Newswire, prnewswire.com, July 1, 2014, https://www.prnewswire.com/news-releases/survey-more-than-half-of-employees-have-worked-for-a-micromanager-265359491.html.

to come across as too prescriptive. But this is exactly *why* we set expectations with our teams about how we want to work up front—so we don't have to continually nitpick at things later.

Expectations outline how we want things to be done based on how we like to work *and* what we think is necessary to run an effective business that achieves our goals. Both different, both important.

Here are examples of each category:

*How we like to work*

- Business hours
- Working from home versus in-office
- Color coding, file naming, folder structures

*Running an effective business*

- How we communicate with clients, turnaround times on client communication
- How we prep for and move things forward before and after meetings
- How we track work and time

They can also take shape as working norms—for example, how do you want to come together as a team, how do you want to communicate, how do we show up for our clients? Mapping out all of this up front and sharing with your team members that this is *how* work gets done in this company avoids having to continually remind people to do it later.

## Chapter 4

I encourage business owners to take the first pass at mapping out expectations, then bring your team members into the fold to discuss the nuances of each, give feedback, add or subtract, etc. Bringing people into the process to co-create and refine working norms and expectations fuels a stronger sense of buy-in and accountability to following them.

Take the ever-rising issue of employees being on cellphones all the time. This is something that business owners with a physical location (restaurant, gym, café, MedSpa, dance studio, etc.) often come to me really struggling with. When no clients are around, it might seem fine to your employees if they continually check their phones. They are always present and friendly when clients come through the doors or are interacting with them, so what's the big deal?

Employees being on their phones all the time creates a few problems. Each time they check their phone, their attention is pulled away from what they're doing, requiring a few minutes of time to re-engage into the work once they go back to it. Even before clients walk in through the door, they might see employees on their phones as opposed to looking present and available to help them, and that doesn't create a welcoming and inviting ambiance. But the biggest issue is that when folks jump to being on their phones the second they finish a task or client interaction, they're not using that time to proactively better your business. This often fuels that frustration as a business owner that you're the only person focused on growing the business or that your team members are only there to collect a paycheck and go home.

How do you tackle this and create a stronger sense of buy-in across our teams? Set expectations about what to do be doing *between* tasks or client interactions. With a MedSpa client, we created a list of all of the "business building" activities team members should be doing when they have downtime—from checking that patient rooms are spotless, to proactively following up with clients who recently visited, to researching trends in the industry, to updating charts for clients. Then, instead of just saying, "Don't be on your phones," the business owner said to her team, "Here are the kinds of activities we do between client appointments," and folks worked their way through the checklist each day. When we framed the expectations in this way, also inviting folks to co-create the list and add other things they do routinely, people were eager to chip away at the tasks on the list. They just needed the expectation to be set. Remember, they can't read our minds.

Thinking about what your expectations are and communicating them to your team so everyone is on the same page sets the stage for a better relationship with feedback as well.

Feedback is one of the toughest skills to nail at work, making feedback conversations awkward, uncomfortable, unhelpful, or infrequent. This is often because we're giving feedback on something that the feedback receiver doesn't totally agree with or understand. I often say the question "Can I give you some feedback?" is the workplace equivalent of saying to someone you just started dating, "Hey, can we talk?" It sends them running for the hills; we don't know what we're about to be hit with.

But this doesn't mean we want to avoid it. A Gallup poll of over 65,000 employees found that companies that provide regular feedback on employees' strengths and development opportunities have an almost

15% higher employee retention rate than those that don't give regular feedback.[5] This means our team members are hungry for feedback and are counting on us to develop the skills to deliver it effectively.

When we map a piece of feedback to a clear expectation, we can give specific feedback about how it relates to that expectation without it feeling personal. Take for example the expectation, "we save all project work on the Google Drive server before the end of each week." If someone didn't save their project work on the Google Drive, you can address that specifically and make a clear ask about what to do next time: "We save all our project work on the Google Drive server before the end of each week, and when you went on vacation and didn't upload your work, Jen wasn't able to cover for you and complete the project. Can you double-check that you've uploaded all of your active work before you log off at the end of each week?"

See how that makes the feedback so much more palatable? You're not implying this person is incompetent or forgetful or a bad employee, you are simply sharing the impact of not doing the thing you set the expectation on. The feedback doesn't feel personal or arbitrary because it's based on something you've already talked about.

If you had never set the expectation that all work should be uploaded to Google Drive before the end of each week and gave feedback that a problem resulted because of someone not doing it, they'd be sitting there wondering, "Why didn't you ever say that's what you wanted?"

---

5. "What these 3 statistics can tell us about employee expectations," Kineo, learningnews.com, June 2, 2021, https://learningnews.com/news/kineo/2021/what-these-3-statistics-can-tell-us-about-employee-expectations.

Set the expectation up front, and you will always have something to point back to. In this example, we're simply reminding the employee about the agreed expectation to upload their work to Google Drive, and it's not personal or nitpicking.

## Expectations Bust Assumptions

Expectations allow us to avoid assumptions—both assumptions made by our team members and by ourselves.

I was managing a program manager who was great at building relationships with her team members and did a good job of keeping work on track, but she was falling short when it came to documenting her own work (e.g., writing up a proposal for how she would solve a problem, tracking things consistently in spreadsheets, capturing post-project learnings). In this company specifically, documentation was a major factor in how her performance was evaluated, so I knew I had to course-correct.

"Joan, I hear all great things from your team about your work, and the projects are going really well, but I'm missing seeing the documentation that goes along with everything."

"Oh, I don't need to play that game."

Taken aback by her statement, I paused and asked, "What do you mean by *game*?"

"In this company, everyone wants you to create documents about everything. Went to the bathroom, here's a report. Had a meeting, here's a report. I'm not playing that game."

## Chapter 4

It was clear no one had ever set expectations with her about why documentation was important.

"Totally get where you're coming from," I said. (Alright, if I'm being honest, I only *kind of* got it, but it wasn't worth pushing on.) "But project documentation is the evidence that you did the work that you said you did. I believe you did it, but when performance review time comes and I have to advocate for you and everyone else has a boatload of documents showing how they approached problems, tracked progress, and got buy-in from different teams and you don't, I have no way to defend your work. Maybe it is a game, but it's one you have to play if you ever want to get promoted."

"Oh..."

At that moment she realized the assumption she had that documentation wasn't important was limiting her career.

"Let me send you a few examples of project documents so you can see what I mean. It doesn't have to be complicated, but you do have to do it."

I sent her some examples, and over the next few days, she started creating documentation for all of her projects, emailing me with the subject "Merry Christmas" and a link to the document each time she finished one. She got totally into it and ended up having the best documentation of anyone on my team.

As for the assumptions we make about our teams and businesses—exploring the expectations set, or not set, can help us bust through those as well.

One of my salon-owner clients recently came to me concerned that her rebooking rates were flat, even on the decline. Could it be the services she was providing? Issues clients had with the staff? She hadn't heard any concerns and clients were always happy when they came into the spa, so that didn't seem to be the issue. Something else was going on.

We started to discuss expectations around employees talking to clients about rebooking, and it hit us like a ton of bricks: there weren't any. If the employee administering a service or the person at the front desk remembered, they'd ask clients to rebook; but it wasn't happening consistently. So we decided to set a new expectation with everyone on her team: *anyone* who interfaces with a client at any point—the person walking the client to their station, the person administering a service, the person collecting payment at the end of their appointment—asks them when they'd like to rebook their next service.

The team was immediately on board. It was an easy request because of course employees wanted clients to come back in; and it wasn't as if they hadn't wanted to ask about rebooking, they just hadn't realized it was part of their job. Once they started asking about rebooking regularly, the rebooking rates started to shoot back up.

When reflecting on this situation, I was reminded of how important it is to take a step back and re-examine expectations before we make assumptions. When something goes awry in our business, it can be easy to want to jump in and change a bunch of things to get it back on track. But when we start changing multiple things at once, it's hard to tell what the root of the problem was and if we actually had to change so many things. A lot of times, the missing link is simply a gap in communication. A question to ask ourselves when we encounter something like clients not extending contracts or in this case with rebooking is "What expectations have I set around this activity?" If the answer is "none yet," the fix is simple.

Set expectations with your teams about educating your clients as well. Many of our businesses offer services that are complimentary with other products or services they sell. All of your employees and team members should know what these are and how they work together to help your clients get to their desired results faster. Clients tend to assume everyone on your team knows about everything your company offers—this means we have to set the expectations with our teams that they do know about all the things our company does and offers and how products or services work together to drive better results.

This is especially true for companies that don't have roles like account or project managers, where clients might be interfacing with different roles within your team. For example, with a MedSpa client, we set the expectation that team members performing injectable services understand the aesthetic services and vice versa so they can speak to how pairing them achieves better results. This both creates a better outcome for your clients and an opportunity to increase the value of that client. It also helps people bring more innovative ideas around growing the business because people understand the full surface area of your business, not just their one piece of the puzzle.

## Where do we go *right* with setting expectations?

Map out all the things that would be helpful to spell out about how you want your business to be run, thinking specifically about any assumptions potentially being made. The more comprehensive the better.

## Why Are Expectations So Important?

Expectations are the recipe to scale, plain and simple. And I don't even mean that as a metaphor; they are the *literal* recipe that enables you to create a repeatable process or system or business model or customer experience or you-name-it across your company.

Let's say you own a coffee shop that is crushing it and you want to open a second location. While the fantastic pastries and delicious fair-trade coffee is part of the success, there is so much more that makes your coffee shop special. The energy the employees bring, the music played, the organization of the space, the silly doodles on the chalk menu, the frequency the garbage is taken out, the freshness of the coffee, the sampling of the pastry of the day. These are all specific and intentional things you established through expectations with your team members that you want to see reproduced in the next location. Likely much of it came together as you went along, and the exercise of mapping out what makes your coffee shop the unique place it is (including all of the little details, nuances, and expectations that go along with it) will ensure you can create that same magic in your next location.

Not only do expectations create a consistent experience for our customers and clients, they create consistency for our employees as well. Write down and communicate the overarching expectations you have for all team members as a whole—essentially, what it means to be part of your company. This is a great place to articulate aspects of the culture you want everyone to embody and uphold. It's also an opportunity to get a little more explicit on some of the policies: "return to office," work tracking, business hours, dress code (if applicable), etc. Establishing these things as team expectations that everyone subscribes to shifts them from feeling nitpicky to "just the way we do things here."

Then, outline any specific expectations for each role. These are the things *outside* of the job description or responsibilities, things like greeting clients in a certain way, client intake process, etc. Again, mapping this out means that *every* team member who joins your company in that particular role will follow the same process and understand what to do, resulting in employees being treated equitably and everyone interfacing with your employees to have the same experience.

## Diagnostic Questions

When figuring out what to set expectations about, consider the following questions:

- What are some of the things that are important to you about how the work gets done?
- What do you wish people would just do (e.g., keep you in the loop, not come to you unless there are problems, be proactive, ask you first, etc.)?
- What questions are you answering over and over and over again?
- Where do you feel like people are missing something important or missing the mark?
- What are some of the norms around work hours, communication, keeping you updated, chain of command, etc.?
- If you have managers or people leaders, what are specific expectations you have of these roles?

## It's Not Too Late!

Also known as, but I thought I *did* set expectations . . .

We can answer all of the above, making things super clear, and yet still feel the "why don't they just . . ." feels.

When that happens, set them again.

Because this stuff is so clear in our minds, we might think it only needs to be said once. But if we're not seeing the follow-through, we have to check back in with our teams.

A helpful framing for this conversation is to reiterate the expectation and ask folks if there is anything that didn't make sense or if they have any feedback they want to share. For example, back to that Google Drive situation, if a team member continues to not save their work on the server, it could be helpful to understand what's getting in the way.

Saying something like, "Hey, we talked about putting all project documentation on the server by Friday end of day, but it's been a few weeks, and I haven't seen it up there. Is there something we could change about this process to make it easier?"

The answer to this question might surprise you. They might say, "OMG, I just totally keep forgetting!" or they might say, "Yes, I totally understand—and every time I go to upload my files, the server times out and crashes all my programs." With the former, adding a calendar reminder on Friday EOD could be the solution, and with the latter, the team member might need a new work computer. We don't know what's getting in the way if we don't ask.

Expectations are living and evolving things, which is why we want to keep them as an open conversation. This doesn't mean everything is up for grabs, it means we talk about them continually and revisit them when something isn't working or needs adjusting. With that said, expectation setting (and resetting and resetting and resetting) can be one of the toughest areas in the whole Ops Playbook system to tackle, so if you're feeling stuck, head to **liagarvin.com/unstoppable** to sign up for an SOS call to get immediate actions you can try on your team to get everyone on the same page towards meeting those expectations.

**Let's Recap**

- Expectations clarify the way you want things to be done in your business.
- Expectations don't feel like micromanaging when communicated up-front or through a more outcome-based lens.
- Collect feedback on expectations to gain buy-in across the team, and continually consider how you can be more clear if expectations aren't being met.

With clear expectations setting everyone up for success, we can get into the brass tacks.

Let's talk work tracking.

# Make a Lasting Impact in Real Time

The best part about simplifying how work gets done on your team and reducing stress on yourself as a business owner is that the gains are *infinite*.

When we start carving out more time in our days for ease and flow, we see new ideas come to the surface that weren't there before, our team members are happier, we are more present with our families, we're kind of better people all around.

Wouldn't it be awesome if the employees were set up for success like this in *every* business we went to or worked with? What if small business owners didn't have to face closing their doors due to little inefficiencies in their companies that they totally could have resolved if they had the tools?

Then let's spread the word!

If you are enjoying this book so far and see the kind of benefit that can be achieved by applying the tools, would you take one minute out of your day to write a quick review wherever you purchased the book?

Taking sixty seconds to share a review allows me to reach more business owners with these tools and help make the workplace somewhere everyone can thrive.

Thank you in advance for helping build this movement.

It's so much better for you to get the picture of status and capacity than to have no picture, even if you got a great tool that can do a million things. Start with those two dimensions and then build from there.

## Chapter 5
# Work Tracking

The assignment: Present a fully working demo of our product at Build, Microsoft's annual developer conference in three months. The issue: We had *no* idea how far off we were from actually being able to do this. I joined the team in December, and we had to be ready to showcase our work to the world in February; and by my initial assessment, the design team that I was program-managing needed more like three *years* to get it all done. This initial assessment, however, was only based on a hunch because the team had no consistent system for tracking their work.

I rolled up my sleeves and dove in, sitting down with each team member one by one to understand their process for doing their work, how they were tracking what they were working on, and where they were getting stuck.

Good news and bad news.

The good news was there was way more work underway and in progress than designers were getting credit for. A ton of work was being explored, happening, and ready to be handed off to engineering to put into the product.

The bad news was that without a formal system for tracking our work, we didn't have a sense of what needed to be done next, what tasks the designs connected to on the engineering side, and how much work was left. The lack of visibility into how we were working created a rift between design and engineering—with engineering thinking design was working on an island and didn't want to share their work, and design thinking engineering didn't value their craft.

Let's pause the story right there because this is where it connects to so many of the challenges with work tracking that I see in smaller teams as well. We don't have a consistent system for tracking work on our teams and aren't fully clear on what people are working on, then we worry they're working on the wrong things or assume they're not making enough progress on everything. Or, we don't have a consistent system for tracking work so we assume everything is going fine, only to be frustrated when work goes offtrack because we wish someone had said something earlier. The latter is especially problematic for open-ended projects where deadlines can be more fluid. For example, projects like improving team culture, building the social media presence of the company, or optimizing processes within the business where people pick up working on them when they have spare time.

Tracking tasks in some kind of formalized system is imperative for running a business. Without it, you have no idea the overall status of work, can't get a sense of workload on each team member to know when people are at overcapacity (informing if you need to hire more people and when), can't anticipate when things will be finished, and don't know how long work takes to complete so it's hard to know you're pricing your services correctly (usually resulting in leaving money on the table). In addition, without tracking work, we often miss the step of scoping the work or defining what a project even includes, and with those open-ended projects that I mentioned, it becomes difficult to know when they're completed.

And I don't mean multiple systems, I mean a single system. One place we can go wrong on teams is having multiple systems to track work that don't all fit together—spreadsheets, notes apps, Trello boards, and everyone's favorite, Post-Its.

I worked on several teams in the past where I was one of multiple project managers managing work across a shared pool of designers. This is likely a common scenario for you agency owners reading this. On teams where there was no formal system for tracking work, I would use the system that I thought of, and the other project managers would use the system they thought of. It worked great for each of us. It worked terribly for the designers who had to track their work completely differently depending on which one of us project managers they were working with.

Having to manage two or more different systems in their heads was a huge cognitive load for the designers, making it difficult to prioritize their work. Not only that, using different systems meant we couldn't get a unified view on the status of all the work happening in the agency. Without this view, the project managers were always having to renegotiate timelines with each other or ask designers to put in extra hours to finish something when deadlines fell on the same day so we wouldn't have to let down the client.

If you are managing a set of account managers or project managers or people responsible for tracking work, consider setting an expectation that they work together to come up with a system everyone commits to using across the team to minimize thrash.

The time and money that could be recouped from mitigating everything in the last few paragraphs could literally buy you a three-month all-expense-paid trip to the dream destination of your choice, where you would peacefully lay on the beach sipping Mojitos, not having to think about any of this stuff.

## Where do we go *wrong* with work tracking?

Not having a single, consistent system for tracking work or tasks, resulting in assumptions that the work is way more offtrack than it is (and people don't get credit for what they've been doing), or that it's way more on track than it is (resulting in surprises when deadlines are missed or people feel overwhelmed with workloads).

**So What Do We Do About It?**

Looking at my design team back at Microsoft, two things were needed: a simple system for tracking work and the repairing of relationships with the engineering and product teams. The best part was tracking our work would get us 80 percent of the way there on the relationship with the other teams because we'd be able to clear up some of those assumptions causing the tension.

Kicking off the effort to start tracking tasks, I knew I'd have to be tactful with my approach. People weren't just going to enter their tasks into a system because I said so; I'd have to paint the picture of why it was important and what was in it for *them*. Many people on the team had been working on the product for years, and the milestone that was coming in three short months was our moment to share with the world what folks had been working so hard on. But we didn't know how far off we were, creating stress for ourselves and the other teams who were depending on us.

Not only that, without a clear sense of our workload, we were getting left out of conversations around product direction and strategy. Tracking our work would allow us to not only have a better handle on the workload and what was doable in the next three months, if we connected our design tasks to the engineering tasks, we'd ensure they couldn't move forward without design being in the conversation. I explained all of this and said I'd make it as easy as possible. I'd enter all the known work for the next month into the tool, and team members could enter new tasks as they came up. The team got on board. Why? Because *their* needs, *their* concerns, and *their* goals were at the center.

Over the next few weeks, the results surprised even me, in a good way. As people started entering tasks into the system, it started forcing conversations around scope and timeline that weren't happening as regularly before. And as I hoped, it was creating a bridge between the design and engineering teams because we could now look at the work holistically. I saw designers proactively adding tasks to the system, eager to check them off when they were done, proactively reporting on work progress. We made it to demo day with all work completed on time, and it was a smashing success.

I built it, and they came.

When I talk about work tracking, most people's corporate bureaucracy radars fire on and they want to stop inviting me to meetings. Hey, this happened even when I was *in* the corporate world. It's because work tracking systems are usually too heavy handed and try to solve too many problems. Fortunately, when I say "work tracking system" I mean to find the *simplest* solution that you can align around company-wide that solves two problems:

1. Status of work (where are things at)
2. Capacity of the team (how busy are people)

People often ask me how to select the right tool for your team. Remember, the first criterion is to pick something *everyone* agrees to use. A Post-It plus a spreadsheet does not equal success.

In the Microsoft example, we entered our tasks into the same tool the engineering team was using so we could have shared visibility across all work. If you don't have one place to see the status of everything, then you haven't solved your problem. That's most important. This is where you might encounter a rub on your team, one person likes using a notes app, someone else Trello, someone Asana, and so on. People might ask why it matters to have it all in one system if they're managing their workload independently and getting things done on time.

To run your business, forecast, plan, shift priorities to respond to competitive forces, you-name-it, you need to have a unified view. Some people will have to give up the system they were using that worked for them, and that's part of setting expectations about working in your team. And by framing it in what's in it for *them* to track their work in a single system (reducing bottlenecks, celebrating accomplishments, reducing burnout, being able to focus people on the right work, paying overtime, evaluating promotion readiness, knowing when to hire more people), the conversation about retiring their existing process gets a lot easier.

When trying to figure out what system to use, be mindful of getting carried away by all of the awesome things a tool can do. Sure, there are many tools and products out there that can track a million different things: status, dependencies, budgets, forecasts, resourcing plans, capacity, goal-setting, ending world hunger—all in one place. But a lot of times, we start using a complicated piece of software, struggle with teaching everyone how to use it, everyone uses it inconsistently so we can't reap any of the benefits of the more complex features of the tool, and then it fizzles out. We feel like we wasted our time and money, and the team gets skeptical about the idea of work tracking, making it harder to use a system in the future. Yep, I've been there all too many times.

This is why I'm such an advocate for simplicity. It's so much better for you to have a view into status and capacity than to have no picture at all, even if you purchased a great tool that can do a million things. Start with those two dimensions and then build from there.

## Where do we go *right* with work tracking?

Paint the vision of why we track work and what's in it for your team members, and they will get on board. Then choose one simple system where you can track the status of work and capacity of each team member.

## Task Tracking vs. Time Tracking

I'm just gonna call it—most people are terrible at estimating how long work takes for them to do. When I was on the Hololens team building the first product of its kind, I asked a 3D artist to give me an estimate of how long it would take him to create a 3D model of a human.

"How would I know?" he said. "I've never built a holographic computer before." Cool, thanks, bro.

This person was a 3D artist who came from the gaming world, and he had built hundreds of 3D models of humans before.

"Imagine you're building this for a game, what would you have said to your producer in the past? One day, one week, two weeks? Gimme some kind of idea, and then let's talk about what's different about this project that we can factor into the estimate," I replied.

If someone gives you grief about not being able to estimate time, ask them to estimate based on *similar* work in the past as a starting point. Then ask them to calculate (with a timer if needed), just this first time, how long it takes to do the task in this situation and compare the results. I did this when I start my podcast *Managing Made Simple* and was managing all the tasks myself from recording to editing to creating videos to writing show notes and LinkedIn articles. I had never made a podcast before, so I had no idea how long the whole process would take. But I tracked how long each step took for the first few episodes and got insight into what was taking up the most time so I could look for ways to automate or outsource it.

## Chapter 5

Quick sidenote: While this chapter is for the most part about tracking work for your team members, I cannot stress enough how important it is to understand how you are spending your *own time* as a business owner. If you perform services, you likely have a high billable rate you could be putting against that service delivery, yet a lot of times, as business owners we get stuck working on administrative tasks because we think there's no one else to take it on, or maybe we're just used to doing it. When I tracked how long the podcast was taking me, it was eye-opening. The podcast was really important to me to be doing, but I didn't have to do all the steps in the process myself. As opposed to getting hyper-fixated on the audio editing and annoyed at the sound of my own voice resulting in editing a ten-minute episode taking over an hour, I could hand off that piece and refocus my time on serving Ops Playbook clients.

One of the biggest challenges business owners come to me with is managing their own time, and if we're not good at that, it becomes really difficult to manage our team members' time. Use whatever system you implement on your team for yourself as well. It will help you stress-test it, understand what works and doesn't work about the system, and get a handle on your own project status and overall capacity.

In my opinion, task tracking outweighs time tracking, but that doesn't mean we don't need a sense of how long tasks take to be completed. We have to understand what is included in a task and how long those different elements take so we know how many tasks a person can complete in a certain time frame.

If you're finding work in your team continually taking longer than estimated or someone on your team continually being pulled in different directions and not finishing things, timesheets can be really helpful for determining how someone is spending their time and what the issue is.

A concern I often hear from business owners about tracking time at the more granular level is worrying again about coming across as a micromanager or like they are monitoring people too closely. This interpretation is in the eye of the beholder and can be mitigated by the framing you use to talk about why you're tracking time and what you do with the information you find. If you use time sheets to ensure your team members aren't working way more hours than they're being paid for, that you're not undercharging clients for services, or to understand when you need to hire more people to relieve some pressure on the existing team—then timesheets are a great thing. If it is perceived that you're using timesheets to try to catch people not working hard enough or spending too much time on simple tasks, then of course team members are going to resist them.

And with that said… please don't use timesheets in place of feedback conversations. If you have an inkling that someone is not spending their time on the right things, have a conversation about it—discuss your expectations for the task or project, ask them to give you a sense of how long the work should take, then give them an opportunity to meet that expectation.

If timesheets feel appropriate for your business, try the gist of this framing to disarm any concerns from your team members:

"We have had an influx of work lately and are going to experiment with tracking time at a more granular level for the next two to three months. The goal of tracking time is to ensure we understand all the work that goes into completing a project and how long the different pieces take. This allows us to ensure you're not over capacity, you're being paid fairly for the work you're doing, and we're charging our clients the right amount for the services offered. We also can get a better sense of where there are gaps in staffing so we can hire more team members to lighten the load."

Then, I like to spell out the level of detail that should be tracked (15/30/60-minute increments, naming conventions, etc.) so everyone is doing it consistently.

Messaging it in this way leads with the benefits *to your team members* so they see that any extra lift of remembering to enter their time in a system is worth it to them personally.

## But Wait, There's More

A question I get from business owners all the time is "How do I know my team members are working on the right things?" Short answer is *work tracking*, and the longer answer is by really understanding the story your work tracking system is telling you.

The COO of a marketing firm I worked with recently came to me concerned because his managers felt really underwater and overwhelmed with their workloads. Initially we figured the managers must be putting in twelve-hour days based on the picture they painted. But as we dug into the task-tracking system and the time the managers had reported, the data showed they were only working about six or seven hours (add in an hour for lunch or breaks, and that was pretty standard).

As we talked more about what was going on, it struck him that his managers always responded to emails within minutes, no matter what time of day it was. They operated almost as if they were on-call. That resonated with me because that's always how I've worked, and in the past it had led me to feel burned out in a job. Many of us check our phones when we're on the couch watching a show and reply to an email to move the ball forward or cross something simple off the to-do list. Checking in here and there might seem like no big deal. But when our team members get hooked on *always* checking, they might feel like they can never step away, or like they never really turn off work mode, even if they don't realize that's what they're doing.

These little tasks that we knock off our list while we're watching TV or eating breakfast are *still work,* and it's important to account for them that way so we have a real sense of our team members' full workloads. For the marketing firm, once the team started entering all of these little tasks into the system, we saw that they really were working around the clock and they needed to load balance. We also saw they were picking up tasks here and there that were being dropped by other team members, showing us they needed to have conversations about roles and responsibilities and potential needs for additional staffing.

With hourly employees, this extra time can add up *real* quick.

For one of my MedSpa clients, this same situation of a team member picking up little odds and ends tasks here and there was resulting in a lot of overtime hours. The business owner noticed that their office manager was entering overtime hours week after week and continually saying she couldn't get all of the work done that she needed to do. The owner was happy to pay overtime if all the extra work was necessary and helping the business but wasn't excited to pay it if it was a result of the office manager working on the wrong things all day. We only got to the bottom of it when the team started tracking work.

This was a stickier situation for this company in particular because the business owner had asked the office manager to track her work a number of times in a simple spreadsheet to start with, and week after week it wasn't happening. When a new team member started who would be working with the office manager at the same location, we saw it as the perfect opportunity to re-engage on the work tracking.

Instead of making the office manager feel singled out, we asked both the office manager and the new team member to track their work since both of their schedules weren't tied to client appointments. We also framed the reasoning for tracking her work in terms of what the office manager wanted because, I'm telling you, it is the best way to get people on board with doing something new. The office manager wanted to focus on more strategic work but said her time was always being taken up with little fires to put out throughout the day, leaving only evenings to tackle the more interesting work. The business owner explained to the office manager that the only way she could hire someone to offload some of the tactical work was if she understood what all the work consisted of and how long it was taking to get done—hence why work tracking was so important. Otherwise, everyone would just be guessing, and it would be impossible to know what to take off the office manager's plate.

The combination of seeing work tracking was in her *own* best interest, and tracking her work along with another employee did the trick. After the first day of work tracking, I kid you not, I got a text from the business owner that the MedSpa had a 200 percent increase in sales, all because being conscious of what they were working on focused them around working on the most important things.

Not only that, with a clear sense of all the little things she worked on each day, the office manager and business owner could sit down together to better prioritize the work, clearly delineating between what actually had to get done each week and what wasn't as important, removing the need for overtime hours.

## Diagnostic Questions

When thinking about tracking work, consider the following questions:

- How do you know who is working on what?
- Where do people track what they're working on and how long it takes?
- What are the forums where your team comes together? What's the agenda?
- How are actions tracked between meetings?

## Speaking of Optimizing Time . . .

When was the last time you had a meeting run over by fifteen minutes? Last week? Yesterday? Today? It seems like no big deal. The team went on a tangent about another topic, or folks got sidetracked talking in the coffee area and the meeting started late, or you had a phone call in the middle of the meeting and had to step away so it took longer to get through everything on the agenda. All totally common and totally valid.

Chapter 5

But.

Oh, by now you knew there would be a *but*. ;)

When we multiply this "dead time" across the hourly rate we're paying our employees, plus what our "business owner" rate is per hour, having a few meetings each week run over by ten to fifteen minutes can really add up.

Let's do the math. Say you have ten team members each averaging about $25 per hour, and two of your meetings each week run over by fifteen minutes. As a CEO, let's estimate your hourly rate (or an hour of your time is worth) is about $350. (I'm internationally being super conservative here.)

Take that thirty minutes per week, multiply it by the number of team members and their hourly rates, add that thirty minutes multiplied by your hourly rate, multiplied by four weeks in a month, and you get $1,200 per month, or $14,400 *per year* in money going down the drain.

Worse than this are meetings that go a full thirty minutes or hour, or even longer, that wrap up and everyone kind of looks around and thinks, "Was this meeting even necessary?" And for most of us, this isn't just one meeting—it's one of the eleven to fifteen meetings businesses have *per week* on average, according to research by productivity software Fellow.[6]

This happens all the time. There's a miscommunication in the Slack so you throw a meeting on the calendar to hash things out. There's a

---

6. Brier Cook, "Do You Know the Average Time Spent in Meetings?" Fellow, fellow.app, February 28, 2023, https://fellow.app/blog/meetings/do-you-know-the-average-time-spent-in-meetings/.

weekly recurring meeting that you don't totally think has value, but you assume someone must think it does because everyone keeps showing up, so you keep it on the calendar. You have a routine check-in with your managers who have a lot of work on their plates and are feeling overwhelmed, so the check-in turns into a circular venting session that doesn't lead to any solutioning. We all have the situation that happens on our teams that results in that same question: "Was this meeting even necessary?"

To solve both the meeting overages and needs for meetings, I suggest setting up some working norms around meetings in general. With the teams I support, as tactical as it can seem, this is where we get some of the most recurring cost savings because so many of us spend so much of our time in meetings.

Norms could include deciding the following:

- What constitutes a meeting—meaning, you establish some kind of criteria that has to be met in order to bring people together in a meeting
- How you determine meeting attendees, ensuring meetings don't get too big or have people there who are just spectators
- How information and decisions get communicated from meetings to the broader team to avoid big meetings masking a bigger issue with the cascading of information on your team
- What materials are prepared and shared before a meeting and by when—at the very least, a meeting agenda (I don't love to prescribe, but *every meeting should have an agenda!*), and if needed, pre-read materials, reports that will be discussed, etc.

*Chapter 5*

- How you capture ideas or topics that come up within the meeting but aren't related to the agenda of the meeting so you can go back to them without derailing the current meeting, sometimes this is called a "parking lot"
- How actions, next steps, follow-ups are tracked after a meeting

Now, I 100 percent do not advocate getting rid of meetings altogether. This is sometimes where people's heads go when I talk about reducing the overhead of meetings, and getting rid of meetings or trying to solve everything through text message will result in way more wasted time than the $1,200 per month from the fifteen-minute meeting overages.

I recently met with a team whose managers were frustrated because in an effort to reduce time spent in meetings, folks were having discussions about major philosophical questions about their product strategy and vetting decisions all through instant message. They said if you glanced away from the endless rolling chat, you might miss seeing that your project deadline got moved by three months. Folks ended up taking longer to get their work done because they were so distracted by the conversations happening in chat and ended up having to have even more meetings to unwind decisions that people we're all aligned around. This is an extreme example, but it reinforces the point to decide on criteria for a meeting, then only having meetings that meet those criteria.

Between gaining clarity on what is being worked on, understanding how long work takes, and optimizing your meetings, getting a handle on tracking work has the potential to reap hours of savings every single week, allowing you freedom to grow and hire or reinvest time and money into your business.

### It's Not Too Late!

If your meetings are going way over time, you don't have a clear system for tracking tasks, and you know work is taking longer than it needs to, *do not worry*. This is a gift, because now you know what to look out for and can do something about it.

You might be reading this and want to make a lot of changes quickly, and it might be really tempting to buy some super-robust task-tracking software to solve a bunch of problems all at once. Stick to the guidance I shared of solving the two problems of work status and capacity. These two variables will get you 80 to 90 percent of the information you need to make decisions from and won't overwhelm your team by making too many changes at one time. With tracking time, start by asking team members to be more conscious of how long tasks or projects take so they can estimate if finishing work is taking longer or shorter than anticipated.

Adjusting your meetings to be more focused around agenda also doesn't need to remove all the personality from your team. Consider baking in five minutes at the start of meetings to catch up or setting up routine virtual coffee hours to make space for more informal conversations. The goal isn't to make your meetings robotic or all-business-no-fun; it's to avoid the all-too-common situation of aimless or pointless meetings. Not everything can be solved over Slack, email, or text. Meetings are still important. It's all about getting on the same page around what's being discussed, who is covering what, and the expected outcomes of the conversation (e.g., decision, approval, new ideas, updates, etc.).

## Let's Recap

- We can't run an effective business if we don't track work.
- Tracking the status of work and the capacity of team members will give you a solid picture to understand where things are, how long they take, and how much time there is for more work across your team.
- Meetings are one of the biggest black holes of time wasted on teams. Form some lightweight norms to optimize the time spent in meetings (but don't get rid of meetings wholesale!).

Knowing about all the work happening in your team and the bandwidth people have to tackle more work, we can get real about what *you* actually need to be doing versus what you can hand off.

It's time we talk about delegating and decisions.

**Figure out for yourself what kinds of decisions you don't need to be part of, and hand them off. The more you leave in your team members' courts, the more they will learn, figure things out, and bring their own creative ideas to the table.**

# Chapter 6
# Delegating and Decisions

"I have this really cool research project for you that's gonna get you a ton of visibility," said my manager to me one afternoon in our one-on-one meeting.

This was music to my ears. I had been telling my manager for the past few months that I wanted to take on more responsibilities on the team. This was going to be my big moment to stand out and show more impact on the team, to show her that I could step up and lead. I was so excited to hear what she had in mind.

"So for this really important meeting coming up, I need you to find all of the attendees' emails and titles and add to them a spreadsheet."

Ummm . . .

I felt embarrassed that I thought this would be my big break on the team and disappointed in her for positioning this task as some awesome opportunity. I mean how dumb did she think I was?

Pair this with a manager I had a few years later who was completely underwater. She was in all the meetings, commenting in all the Google

Docs, and was the dictionary definition of "spread too thin." Noticing this, I would routinely tell her when I had extra time and ask her if there was anything I could help with, and routinely she would say she'd let me know when she had something. And, you guessed it, she never followed through.

While I appreciated her not just giving me busy work, it was another situation where a manager had delegating all wrong.

Well, right now, we're about to make it all right.

When it comes to delegating work as business leaders, we face all sorts of fears and resistances:

- Not wanting to throw busy work over the fence
- Not wanting to overload our teams with more work when they are already working hard
- Thinking you'll do the task better or faster
- Not wanting to face thinking about how to explain the thing you'd be handing off
- Not having a handle on all of the work on your plate in order to figure out what even to delegate
- Being resistant to trying because you delegated once and it went badly
- Knowing you need to delegate something but don't have a team member right for the job

How many of these resonate for you? Bonus points if it's all of them!

Delegating is tough; we get stuck in all of these fears. When we're busy, the thought of stopping to figure out how to explain something

## Chapter 6

to someone or muscle through their learning curve can feel like too much of an undertaking. Especially when at the moment, you *can* do the thing faster and better.

When you're feeling a lot of pressure from the outside—clients, investors, customers, funders, whoever—it can be easy to want to shield your employees from everything and take on even more work yourself. And to some extent, we should be shielding our team members from some of this. But when we're feeling squeezed, we can fall into the trap of looking at everything on our list as all-or-nothing: we do the whole project and handle every step, or we hand it off fully and lose control. Looking at it this way can put our blinders on to seeing pieces of a task or project that would make great sense to hand off and let someone else lead.

The problem is, and I know you know this deep down, the only way to scale ourselves is if we delegate some of the work we're doing to our team members or external vendors. It's not just because we're only one person and can only do so much in a day, it's also because not delegating cuts us off from seeing how to tackle problems or approach work in a different way than we would, which could drive better results. It also prevents our team members from stepping up as leaders.

Sure, there are some things that are our superpowers; we truly are best in class at them. But it's not all the things. And if you took an honest look at your to-do list, my guess is "superpower tasks" do not constitute *most* of the things you're spending your time on.

This leaves us with two buckets of work: work that could be super exciting and impactful for a team member to take on based on their career goals, skills, and aspirations, and tactical work that kind of sucks but has to get done.

Good news is we can delegate both.

In some respects, delegating tasks can be easier than delegating decisions. Delegating decisions means you not only let go of doing the work itself, it means you also let go of making the calls associated with it.

For our own personal bandwidth as business owners, delegating decisions and tasks might feel similar. But for your teams, being able to make decisions about the work they are responsible for is of utmost importance. They have to feel autonomy in order to feel like their work matters, like they matter. When you take away this autonomy by asking your team members to run every decision by you, you're signaling to them that you don't trust them to make good calls on their own. This slows work down because that team member can't move at their pace; they have to wait for you at each step. And it's demoralizing to them because they feel like you don't think they are capable of making even low-level decisions.

## Where do we go *wrong* with delegating tasks and decisions?

Delegating something trivial and dressing it up as something more important, resisting delegating altogether, or being involved in every low-level decision. All of these behaviors show your team members you don't trust them with more responsibilities or to make the calls in areas they are responsible for.

## So What Do We Do About It?

Delegating is our vehicle to be able to both focus our time and energy around our highest and best use, and it empowers our team members to take on more responsibility. It's a tool to bring new ideas and perspectives into solving problems, which often leads to better results than if you just did everything yourself.

Even if folks are finding their footing and something you've delegated takes a little longer to get right at first, the process of doing it lays a foundation for you to be able to move faster in the future because you have freed up your time to focus on something else. And if you're still not convinced of its value, research by Gallup shows that CEOs who delegate effectively see 33% higher revenue than those who don't.[7] So yeah, let's get delegating.

Delegating can include handing off high-impact, career-growing and visibility-building opportunities that align directly with the goals of your team members; and it can include handing off tactical work that you just don't have time for. The high-impact stuff is easier to delegate because we can paint a picture for our team members how taking this thing on is *directly* in service of them accomplishing a goal they have. Through building relationships with our team members in our one-on-ones, listening to them as they share about their interests and goals, and having career conversations, we get to know the kinds of projects or responsibilities that would be meaningful to delegate.

In the past when I knew a manager really understood where I wanted to go in my career and had their radar out for opportunities and projects that would help me get there, I was eager to take on more work. With these situations, I always try to connect the dots for people. For example, "In our last career conversation, you mentioned wanting

---

7. Sangeeta Bharadwaj Badal and Bryant Ott, "Delegating: A Huge Management Challenge for Entrepreneurs," Gallup, news.gallup.com, April 14, 2015, https://news.gallup.com/businessjournal/182414/delegating-huge-management-challenge-entrepreneurs.aspx.

to build up your skills in marketing and get involved in projects in that space. I'd love for you to take on overseeing our spring Instagram campaign. Here is what success looks like for that. [Follow with setting clear expectations]." Connecting the dots shows our team members we were listening to them when they shared what was important to them and that we are continually keeping our eye out for opportunities to help them accomplish their goals. It builds trust, strengthens your relationships, and is a great way to show recognition.

This doesn't mean we can't delegate the tactical stuff, especially if it's taking up a lot of your time that would be better spent on higher revenue-producing activities. Let's just all agree that if we're delegating something tactical, we'll call it what it is and not put lipstick on the pig.

I had another manager years ago who needed me to jump in last minute on a series of executive meetings and take notes because I had some bandwidth and no one else on the team was available to do it. She came to me and said she knew notetaking was not something I should be doing or spending time on, but she really needed my help to step in and be the note-taker for three meetings. Because she acknowledged that it wasn't something I should be doing and time-boxed it to the three meetings, I was happy to do it.

If you're struggling to figure out what to delegate, one simple tip is to start with the kind of work you don't like doing: the things that keep you up at night, the things that take you so much longer than they take someone else.

Years ago, I was managing a project manager who loved planning events. I, on the other hand, hated and continue to hate planning events. The thought of it instantly fills me with panic and dread. I mean, what if no one shows up, what if everything goes wrong, what if everyone hates the event and then me by extension. You name it, it will flash through my mind at 3 a.m. That, and that dumb thing I said to my crush in seventh grade.

Our team had to plan a big event to showcase some tech demos, and I was incredibly relieved that I had a person on my team who was eager to take charge. But at first, because I was so filled with all of these worries, I held onto the reins way too tight. I'd look at the project plan and ask if she had thought about this, that, and the other thing; all apparently things that someone who *liked* planning events would never be worried about for more than five seconds.

After scheduling our third review to go through the plan, she said to me, "Hey, I've done all of this before. I know that events stress you out, but I love planning events. None of this stuff worries me." It was a wakeup call that I had handed off the project but had not delegated the decision-making, resulting in me stressing out the both of us. Here I was asking questions thinking I was being helpful to her, but in reality I was just alleviating my own worries. As a result, I was slowing her down and making her feel like I didn't trust her with the project.

In that moment, it hit me that I had to let go—but I didn't have to let go without making a plan for what made sense as far as check-ins and updates. We decided that weekly updates would be plenty, and between meetings she'd email me right away if there were any places where she was getting stuck. We also talked about what success looked like for the event, alleviating my worries that we might be imagining two different things. And with no surprise whatsoever, her version of success was *way* better than what I had in mind. Of course it was, she was the expert.

This conversation allowed me to step away and really let her run with the planning, and as she promised, the event went off without a hitch.

When we're struggling to delegate decisions or responsibilities, one of the easiest mitigations is to ask the other person what their plan is. Our assumptions are often where we get most stuck, and if we talk through the plan and agree on what success looks like, it is so much easier to let go.

With decisions specifically, ask your team members what criteria they're using to make a decision, what they're factoring in, what perspectives they're considering. This allows you to see if they're checking around all corners you would so you can comfortably hand off that decision. If the decision is something super trivial, consider if you even need to discuss the criteria at all. In most cases, just let it go.

A design firm owner I was working with was finding himself as a bottleneck around decisions, with his team members often waiting for his response to move forward on something. His email inbox, Slack, and text messages were flooded with questions, and he felt like he could never get ahead and knew he was slowing his team down.

He knew he was too much in the weeds, and as we dug into all the places he was spending his time, it was clear that he had inadvertently set the expectation that all decisions had to go through him. He was a fantastic manager to his team members, they all loved him, and people were really happy in their jobs. But they had all gotten into a rhythm, especially from growing from four to eight to fifteen team members really quickly that he had to make all of the calls, big and small.

We went through the decisions he worried most about slowing down and found three places that he realized made absolutely no sense for him to be a part of—budget approvals of less than $500, social media hashtags for posts, and designing the pitch proposals for new business. He identified who on the team was the right person to take each of these on, handed off the decisions, and was able to reclaim three hours of time *every single week*. This business owner was billing high-paying clients for creative direction time at $850 per hour and could now work with clients three more hours each week, or twelve hours every month—an extra $10,200 per month for the business overnight.

Figure out for yourself what kinds of decisions you don't need to be part of, and hand them off. The more you leave in your team members' courts, the more they will learn, figure things out, and bring their own creative ideas to the table. It also fuels the ownership mindset that results in proactive problem solving.

## Setting Expectations Is the Secret Sauce

You might have noticed the theme of expectation-setting coming through as I talk about delegating, and it's because it is the secret sauce to letting things go. Delegating goes badly when you hand something off without clarity on how to do it or how you want things to go. On the flipside, it goes swimmingly when you set clear expectations, including any nuances to how you want the task to be performed (within reason), when you want to check in on progress, criteria that are being considered to make a decision, and what success looks like.

All of these things are discussed through an expectation-setting conversation; and all of this should be sufficient to fully hand something off and not check back in every fifteen minutes. If you're finding yourself needing to check in over and over, it means there are more expectations to be set. Asking your team member to repeat back to you what the plan is and share what open questions they have can be a good way to check for understanding.

When I say, "nuances to how you want the task to be performed," I don't mean giving someone a list of steps that have to be followed exactly. Sure, if someone is new to the team or if it's the type of task that follows a specific protocol for safety or something, then a checklist might be appropriate. But if it's a creative or open-ended task, aligning on what success looks like and some general preferences should be sufficient. In either case, setting the context of why certain steps are important shows your team member there is a reasoning behind any prescriptiveness as opposed to you just being controlling.

With the event planning example, a nuance I might have shared was learnings I had from running the event in previous years—things like food people liked or didn't like, ways we advertised the event that got people to sign up for it in advance, or the way the executive team asked to be updated. You can share examples and ideas and suggestions but ideally still with the invitation for your team member to bring their own creativity to the project.

Delegating is a great opportunity to empower someone to step up and be a leader; you don't want to squander it by getting overly prescriptive. If you have a team member you feel like isn't stepping up enough, consider: have you given them enough space or put the invitation out there?

If you are managing managers, have conversations with your managers about what makes sense for them to delegate and then give them space to delegate to their team members by not checking in with them continually on something they've handed off. When I was a manager in the corporate world, what made delegating the hardest was worrying my manager would come to me with questions about a project one of my team members was working on and I wouldn't be able to answer them. Empower your team member to manage the process, decide together when makes sense for you to check in with them or with the person doing the task, and then respect those boundaries as best you can.

## Where do we go *right* with delegating decisions?

Set expectations with your team member about the task or decision to be made, how you want to check in on progress or what criteria is being used to make the decision, and what success looks like . . . and then let them run with it.

## Diagnostic Questions

Here are some questions to help you figure out what to keep and what to let go of:

- What are the decisions made in your business that *only you* can make?
- What is stopping you from delegating?
- What is your process for making decisions when you have something really big to figure out?
- How are decisions communicated? How would you like team members to communicate decisions to you?

Remember, your team members are always reading between the lines when you interact with them. They can tell when you want more control than you're saying you want. In order to make you happy and be in good favor with you, they'll often follow your lead and back off.

This is why it's so important to be in tune with what you actually *want to be* focusing on and *should be* focusing on from a strategic perspective, and regularly looking for opportunities to offload and delegate. This focus will prevent you from getting in a rhythm where you're doing everything and haven't slowed down because no one said anything, or making too granular of decisions that no one has the freedom to do their jobs.

**It's Not Too Late!**

If you're reading this and realized you're too far in the weeds, share that realization with your team members. A great way to build trust and connection with your teams is acknowledging where you want to do something differently and inviting them to give you feedback on how it's going.

Whenever I find myself too far in the weeds, I like to do a simple time audit, consisting of the following four steps:

1. Look across a one-to-two-week period and make a log of all of the things you are spending your time on.
2. Circle all of the things that *only* you can do. (Be really honest with yourself here, most things should *not* be circled. This is typically three to four things.)
3. Underline all of the things that you would like to delegate but need to hire or train someone to do that work first.
4. Put a box around all of the things that you can delegate right now, and get delegating. What I love about this system is that Step 3 essentially gives you a job description for hiring someone to perform a bunch of responsibilities that you want to get off your plate, or a solid plan of what you'd need to

train someone to take on. Step 4 gives you a list to hand off right away. And once you have that list to hand off . . . go hand it off!

For this exercise, it can be really helpful to get an outside perspective to help you categorize your work into the right buckets and push you to keep the items *you* need to focus on to a minimum. For support with this exercise or anything else when it comes to delegating, head to **liagarvin.com/unstoppable** to schedule an SOS call.

**Let's Recap**

- Delegating tasks and decisions creates opportunities for your team members to step up and do more meaningful work.
- You have the opportunity to save countless hours of your time every single month when you get clear on what to delegate and fully hand it off.
- Delegating effectively requires setting clear expectations around what the work entails when you want to check in about it and what success looks like.

With all of this extra time on your hands, go book a spa day to recharge, because what's coming up next is the last piece of the puzzle—where it all comes together.

Let's talk about evaluating performance.

As the person steering the ship, you can connect the dots between priorities, expectations, and performance and create the holy trinity of everyone in your team working to grow your business.

## Chapter 7
# Evaluating Performance

Having clarity on how you evaluate performance—and making sure everyone on your team is on the same page about what that looks like—is the pinnacle of having expectations met and accomplishing your business priorities. No big deal, we're just talking about the last, and most critical, piece of the puzzle for getting you set up to scale (while reducing overwhelm for yourself as a business owner).

I don't like to play favorites on what's most important, but . . . if your team members don't think a task or responsibility that they're doing is being factored into how they're being evaluated, and by extension factored into what they're getting paid for, they're not gonna do it.

There, I said it.

This is always what surprised me about the corporate performance review systems in companies I worked at and people I coached for so many years on how to represent their accomplishments effectively in performance reviews. The company priorities were one thing and the team priorities another; the expectations of your role were something at most only loosely related, and your performance was based on something else.

Makes zero sense.

Employees felt like they were working toward a moving target or like what they were being asked to do versus being evaluated on was a bait and switch, and it was terrible for fostering collaboration and uplifting other people. All year you'd be told to "work well with others" and "make the team better," and then when it came time for the performance review, the narrative would shift to "What were *your* exclusive isolated contributions with no help from others, only *you* alone?" I got feedback a number of times that I spent *too much time* helping other people be successful, questioning if I spent enough time doing my "real" job.

Yep.

Joke's on them, now helping other people be successful is what I get to do *all day every day*!

As a result? Many people would try to game the system, focusing on only the "promotion-worthy" work and kick the rest to the curb. Team members chased the shiny objects, leaving behind important work like maintaining and improving the quality of existing projects.

Do not do this. As the person steering the ship, you can connect the dots between priorities, expectations, and performance and create the holy trinity of everyone in your team working to grow your business. You have the power in your hands to encourage work that results in great products or services, accelerates your business, and creates a great team culture. The secret is in making clear what that looks like for every job and incentivizing it through how you evaluate performance.

Remember that PR firm CEO who established the priority around the revenue goal and painted the picture of how every role supported accomplishing that? You better believe we established clear performance metrics, directly related to that goal. We set the priority (achieve revenue target), the expectations (specific actions PR account managers can do to acquire or retain clients), and mapped performance to it (performance is accomplishing these individual key performance indicators [KPIs] and goals). And if you remember the results we saw from that example, two account managers brought $13K into the business within weeks.

One of the biggest transformations businesses experience with the Ops Playbook system is getting all team members aligned around their role in growing the businesses, and it all comes down to this chapter.

I said it before and I'll say it again: if a task or responsibility is not part of how your employees think they are being evaluated or what they think they are being paid for, they are not going to do it. I mean, would *you*?

Doesn't mean they aren't working hard or don't care. It means you have not demonstrated that *you value* that task or responsibility. Your team members are following your lead, they are going to double down on the areas *you* focus on. You show what you value by recognizing work in that respective area, rewarding it, giving bonuses and incentives around it. You show it by walking the talk.

Having clear performance criteria that links to expectations and priorities isn't just about growing your business, it's also about employee retention.

The owner of an event production company shared with me recently that she felt like she kept getting things wrong when it came to managing her contract employees and delegating. She had a revolving door of virtual assistants (VAs), and she saw a pattern of people leaving once they hit the three-month mark. She finally found a VA who had stuck around for six months, and the person was crushing it. And the business owner was terrified that person was going to leave.

"Have you shared with her how awesome you think she's doing?" I asked.

"No, I hadn't thought to . . . I guess I really should," she said, realizing there was a huge opportunity here.

When we're working with part-time or contract employees, we can sometimes forget to set performance goals and give the same kind of recognition and appreciation we'd give to full-time employees, losing sight of the fact that people are people and they need to feel appreciated no matter what the work arrangement is.

I encouraged the business owner to share the positive feedback and appreciation directly with the VA and consider setting up a performance target that would result in a raise or incentive for the VA for her continued great work. This would show the VA the kinds of things she was doing that were really knocking it out of the park and that the business owner was invested in her longer term.

## Chapter 7

For our full-time employees, it goes without saying that they need a regular signal of how they are doing and what professional and financial advancement looks like. One of the biggest frustrations I hear from employees on teams is feeling like they don't know where they stand. And if they have no clue when and how performance is evaluated, it's hard to know what you're working toward.

For many of the business owners I talk to and work with, performance conversations happen informally and infrequently. I'd caution against this. Whenever I talk to their employees, folks share that they *want to* know when raises will happen, *want to* understand when they might be promoted or eligible for a title bump, and at the very least *want to* know where they are landing relative to the expectations of their job.

If you're reviewing performance informally to reduce stress on your employees, know that it's likely creating *more* stress. And if you're doing them infrequently because you forget or are too busy, know that *they* probably haven't forgotten.

### Where do we go *wrong* with evaluating performance?

Not connecting the dots between priorities, expectations, and performance and evaluating performance informally and inconsistently.

### So What Do We Do About It?

When I worked at Google, the performance review process was set up where you nominated yourself for a promotion, and then your manager had to support (or not support) the nomination by advocating for it to a committee of their manager peers. If you are wondering if this sometimes resulted in employees asking for a promotion every fifteen minutes, why yes it did.

One breezy springtime morning, in one of our weekly one-on-one meetings, one of my direct reports came into our meeting guns blazin' and said, "I'm ready for a promotion, it's time. I need you to get it for me."

Whelp, this was frustrating on multiple levels. First, because "it's time" isn't a justification for a promotion, and second because "I need you to get it for me" isn't how you ask your manager for support. Even if it was enough to convince me, that wasn't how the process worked at the company.

"I'm hearing that you feel like you're ready for a promotion," I said, "and so I can fully support it and go to bat for you, I'm gonna need you to build the case. Here are the criteria we use to figure out readiness for promotion from your level to the next one. Take the first step of going through this list and identifying examples of projects you've done that correspond to everything on the rubric, and where there are opportunities to take on new projects or responsibilities where you haven't yet met those criteria.

"To get a well-rounded view, talk to three or four people who are in the role you are looking to be promoted into. Ask them what kinds of projects they took on and how they made the leap from your level to the next level. Then let's meet in a few weeks and talk about the plan."

She agreed to this and started outlining her past projects and talking to other people to get their insights. When we met again a few weeks later, she had a clear picture of the aspects of her work that were ready for the promotion and where she needed to focus for the next few months in order to demonstrate readiness. Having *her* do the research and come back with this picture ensured *she* felt accountable to the plan, recognized the gaps, and was taking a proactive role in getting to that next level.

I was then able to give her feedback on some of the areas she thought were closer than they were that still needed more work and recognize and celebrate the places that were already really solid.

The key to success here was putting the accountability ball back in her court—shifting the narrative from "you get it for me" to "here are the ways in which I've demonstrated readiness." Through this lens, she owned her plan to build skills in the areas we talked about, take on new kinds of projects, and get coaching where she needed it.

Your team members *have to* own their career trajectories. You can give them all the support and tools they need to be successful, but at the end of the day, you can't do it for them.

One of the tools that's incredibly helpful for creating clarity and equity in evaluations is a performance rubric. While the thought of having a rubric might seem corporate on the surface, what I'm really talking about here is establishing and communicating expectations. Your team members are going to want to know what they need to do (what metrics to hit, what kinds of projects to work on, etc.) that will result in a promotion, raise, or bonus. A rubric gives them something concrete to work toward. Even folks who aren't motivated by money or titles still want to know where they stand and if they're doing a good job; it's demoralizing when we have no idea.

A simple performance rubric can share examples of what kinds of tasks or responsibilities need to be performed or accomplished to get a promotion or raise. Sometimes they share examples of what it means to meet expectations, exceed, and blow it out of the water in a job. Many of my clients like to adopt a scorecard where we spell out what these criteria are for each kind of role on the "meets," "exceeds," and "transformational" scale. The scorecard can give team members a way to track progress over time.

Rubrics and scorecards aside, again, the important takeaway here is that we aren't accountable for our team members' careers—they are. Create forums where you talk about their career goals and aspirations, and then empower them to own the plan.

Clarity in expectations for performance and what success looks like in a role can also be established through role-specific metrics and KPIs. This worked wonders for that PR firm CEO who set revenue targets for her account managers, and it works great when you want to move the needle on a specific kind of behavior.

A salon owner I met with recently wanted to do a big push on growing her social media following in order to bring visibility to her business and brand. She shared her struggle with getting her stylists to proactively post on social media, and she felt like she had to continually nudge them to post or come up with ideas. To fix this, she decided to gamify it. She created a contest, setting a specific numbers of posts to create each week in order to participate (three times a week). Team members who posted five times a week for a month would be entered to win a gift certificate for a spa day—something she knew everyone would be excited about. Then to incentivize everyone to maintain momentum, if they increased their salon's Instagram account by a certain number of followers, everyone would get a $250 cash bonus.

Once she announced the contest, everyone on the team started thinking about creative ways to capture content. It immediately took the pressure off her in having to come up with all of the ideas herself and resolved the need to continually remind people to post. The key to this salon owner's success wasn't just in doing a contest and in giving prizes, it was in connecting the reward to something that was personally motivating to each person.

## Where do we go *right* with measuring performance?

Establish clear targets or metrics that are based on the company priorities and expectations of people's roles, and evaluate people consistently and at regular intervals.

### Diagnostic Questions

When assessing performance in your company, consider the following questions:

- What does doing a great job look like in your company?
- If someone were to be promoted, what would they have accomplished?
- When do raises or bonuses happen? What are they based on?

- What metrics or KPIs map to each person's roles? Are they aware of these?

## When Should You Measure Performance and What Do You Talk About?

For simplicity's sake, I generally suggest performance being assessed every six months. Annually can feel like too much time has gone by between reviews, and quarterly can feel like you're talking about performance reviews every ten minutes.

Performance conversations are great opportunities to reflect backward (wins and opportunities) and set goals for the next six months. I really like to use the combination of a self-assessment and a manager writeup that the manager and employee meet to talk about. For the self-assessment, the employee puts together a short writeup of their accomplishments, one thing they do well, and one thing they're working on improving. The manager assessment comments on the self-assessment and shares more detailed feedback about the team member's strengths and opportunities.

For larger teams, peer reviews are helpful in evaluating how someone is doing. Just note that with a close-knit team or where people are friends outside of work, sometimes people are not comfortable being candid about someone's "development opportunities," and you don't always get the best data. For teams with multiple managers, I also encourage collecting feedback on the manager performance from team members as well.

With self-assessments, I've found over the years that some team members love writing about their work and making sure to leave no stone unturned, and some find it completely overwhelming and intimidating. Help folks find a middle ground by writing your own self-assessment and sharing it as an example, limiting it to one to two pages so folks see they don't have to write a novel and that the process doesn't need to feel intimidating.

## About Raises and Bonuses

As business owners operating in a continual climate of change and uncertainty, I know we might not always feel like we can commit to giving out annual bonuses or raises, especially with a pre-established dollar amount or percentage. However, Staci Millard, fractional CFO and business mentor recently shared a strategy with me that she uses with her business owners to get the best of both worlds.

Staci helps her clients establish revenue or profit targets, that if met, allow them to give a raise or bonus. She then does the financial forecasting which often highlights they are closer to hitting that bonus target than that business owner realized. With this approach, instead of saying to your team "we can't commit to raises or bonuses this year," you give them a target they can actively all work toward meeting, resulting in transparency in the process, consistency in the message, and everyone going above and beyond to achieve it.

The CEO of a homebuilding company I worked with sets an annual profit target and gives 10 percent of that as bonuses at the end of each year (distributed across the team based on role, tenure, impact, etc.) if they hit the target. She found that doing this creates a strong sense of shared accountability because everyone works as hard as they can in their individual role, and then they work across teams to help folks in other roles so they can all collectively hit that target.

Regardless of the numbers you land on or your method of getting there, I encourage you to set and communicate a consistent timeline for promotions/raises/bonuses; for example, assess in the Q4 performance cycle and pay out on December 15. This way your team members know what to expect and are not spending the whole year wondering if each paycheck is the one where they will see a raise. Bonus (no pun intended), they won't ask you about it every two weeks because they'll know when the conversation is happening.

Controversial opinion moment: Unless it's completely infeasible financially, I think it's critical to give people who are doing a good job a raise *every* year. This isn't even about inflation and cost of living, it's about creating an incentive for staying at your company. My guess is that a goal you have is to make more money every year, so why wouldn't your employees strive for the same? People know that there's always an opportunity to get paid more by changing jobs, and often pay a "loyalty tax" by staying in a company long-term. Be a company that *incentivizes* loyalty.

This is the concept Simon Sinek talks about in *Leaders Eat Last*. Great leaders make sure their team is taken care of before "feeding" themselves; this is what fuels motivation, retention, and the high performance of a team that will lift all boats. Maybe you can't make it rain the way you wish you could, but giving something shows your team members that you value them.

## Spread Recognition Year-Round

Even though I'm mentioning it in the performance chapter, recognizing great work on your team isn't something we want to save for performance conversations alone. A 2023 report by Gallup and Workhuman found that employees who are recognized for their work are twenty times more likely to be engaged in their work than employees who don't receive effective recognition.[8] Twenty times?! Talk about the ability to motivate doing *more with less*.

Effective recognition means making recognition and appreciation specific and meaningful. It's not simply saying "good job" but calling out something specific someone did and why it mattered. It means not operating with a "no news is good news" way of working where you only give feedback when something has gone wrong.

Recognition is rocket fuel for growth and scaling, and not just because it makes us feel warm and fuzzy inside. Recognizing what is working well reinforces the behaviors you want to see more of, resulting in *seeing more of them*.

## It's Not Too Late!

If you're realizing you haven't highlighted enough of the positive lately, right now is the perfect moment to start.

Look across all of your team members and consider each of their strengths and superpowers; what is an area in which they have really been

---

8. "Empowering Workplace Culture Through Recognition," Gallup, gallup.com, accessed December 18, 2023, https://www.gallup.com/analytics/472658/workplace-recognition-research.aspx.

shining lately? Then make it a regular part of your week to highlight and recognize something you are seeing and why it is great. If you're doing this already, you are awesome, keep doing it. And if you're not, you are going to see performance on your team accelerate once you start.

Pro tip from the coaching world is using the tool of acknowledgment or naming a quality you see in someone. We often give feedback with the framing, "*I think* you're great at building relationships." This is nice and all, but do we need the qualifier in front of it? Try naming it directly: "You are a relationship builder," "You are a dot connector," "You are an incredible closer." When the recognition is framed this way, we not only feel seen, we appreciate this quality in ourselves even more, again fueling us to do more of it.

This will also open the door to having those harder feedback conversations because they are anchored in the fact that you appreciate that employee's work on the whole; they trust that you have their best interest in mind.

If you haven't been having performance conversations consistently, there's no time to start like the present. Framing it in terms of wanting your team members to be clear on what success looks like and have an opportunity to share feedback with you as well shows them that performance conversations are in *their* best interest. Remember: everyone feels better when they know where they stand and what a good job looks like. Consider what your criteria is for doing a great job, getting raises and bonuses, and receiving promotions or title changes, and share that with your team. The more we keep folks guessing, the more we risk them looking for a job somewhere where their career trajectory isn't such a mystery.

## Let's Recap

- Connecting priorities, expectations, and performance is the holy trinity for empowering your team members to grow your business.

- Establish clear criteria for evaluating performance and measure it on a consistent timeframe; communicate when promotions, raises, and bonuses will be happening so people aren't wondering.

- Build recognition into your weekly rhythm, finding specific and meaningful examples to share with your team members.

Show up for them in a way that makes it easier for them to put in great work and feel successful, and you will have a team of all-stars who also are vocal brand ambassadors. Not to mention, your job will be so much easier because your team members are bought in.

# Chapter 8
# Make It Simple and Scalable

See? I told you all of this was simpler than you thought.

When we look across all the examples and stories I shared throughout this book, my guess is that even if an example was from a totally different type of company or industry than your company, you could still see yourself in it.

This is because at the end of the day, we're dealing with *people* all figuring out how to work together. The Ops Playbook system works for a multitude of different industries because when it comes to navigating team dynamics, the issues are the same.

I hope that in reading this book you feel less alone, and certainly less like you're the only one struggling with these kinds of challenges. The truth is we all are. All of this is a work in progress where we have good days and bad days. But the bad days are less severe and more infrequent when we have a clear framework to fall back on and when we have created an open line of communication with our teams.

When I talk about the Ops Playbook system, I often share examples of how it saves time and money. That stuff is easy to calculate and helps bring to life what these issues are costing you when you don't resolve them. I mean, when it affects our bottom line, we start to listen.

And if you want to check out how these issues are impacting your own business and get a sense of the time and money left on the table by not solving them, check out my Ops Playbook Savings Calculator at **liagarvin.com/unstoppable**, plugging in data specific to your team.

But the truth is, there is so much more benefit to simplifying the how and streamlining your team operations than just time and money savings.

As a small business owner, your team members are trusting you with their livelihoods and their careers. They are taking a risk joining your company. They are betting on *you*. Show up for them in a way that makes it easier for them to put in great work and feel successful, and you will have a team of all-stars who also are vocal brand ambassadors. Not to mention, your job will be so much easier because your team members are bought in.

How do we show up for our team members? By bringing them along for the process, asking them for feedback, connecting the dots between the work they do and how it supports the overall growth of the business, listening to them, painting a clear picture of what success looks like in their roles, trusting them to make decisions about their work and responsibilities.

We show up for our team members by making it clear what's in it for *them* to work in our company.

This is why when I support companies with the Ops Playbook, the communication to the team of what the playbook is and is meant to do is the most important piece. We have to land the message that the framework and clarity we create is for *them*. It's so *they* see the path to success. Every team member has to know that we recognize that things could be smoother or more clear, and we're rolling this out to ensure we get there. That we're not trying to complicate everything or go corporate. Instead, when we're all on the same page about how to get things done, there is a huge cognitive load lifted that frees us up to work at our best and with so much more ease.

I was once on a team that was in a rough state: plans being agreed to and then second-guessed the moment a meeting was over, people continually debating priorities and goals that had long been decided on, deadlines being missed without any mention of risk or potential delays. Our VP said to me one day, "It feels like everything is so much harder than it needs to be."

It saddened me to hear him say this because while I agreed, unfortunately, *he* was a huge piece of the problem. He wasn't holding people accountable to deadlines or decisions or anything cohesive to come back to. He wasn't being clear in communication and would readily change goals and plans without explanation. The result was confusion, distrust, and an incredible sense of malaise across the whole team.

We all felt what he felt. We were all in the same meetings, reviews, and endless email chains. We all wanted something different.

But he didn't have the tools.

*You* have the tools.

My dream for you is that sixty days after you've implemented this system, you show up to work and see you have recouped enough savings to be able to make that hire that will scale your business, your team members bring new creative ideas to the table because they are clear on how to add the most value, you can finally eat lunch without using your laptop as a placemat.

You have the system, and you have me in your corner waiting in the wings to help you every step of the way.

If you are ready to get support for your business, head to **liagarvin.com/unstoppable** to schedule your free Scale-Up Strategy Call and grab your exclusive bonuses for buying this book. In the conversation, we'll dive into specifics of your business, equip you with a few strategies you can try out right away on your team, and determine which of my programs are a right fit for you and your company. Or if you have a specific challenge you need support on right away, you'll be able to schedule a Team Whisperer SOS call from there as well.

Thank you for joining me on this journey to making managing easier and building your best possible team and most profitable business. I can't wait to see where you go from here.

Don't be a stranger. :)

## Next Steps

Thank you for reading *The Unstoppable Team*. Here are a number of ways to connect with me:

>Visit my **website**: liagarvin.com
>Send me an **email**: hello@liagarvin.com
>Connect with me on **LinkedIn**: LinkedIn.com/in/liagarvin
>Listen to the ***Managing Made Simple*** **podcast**: liagarvin.com/podcast
>Catch my daily tips on **Instagram**: instagram.com/lia.garvin

Head to **liagarvin.com/unstoppable** for all of your resources and freebies:

- Link to **schedule your *free* Scale-Up Strategy Call**
- Link to **schedule a Team Whisperer SOS Call** to get solutions to solve a specific challenge you are stuck in
- Thriving Team Scorecard with **ten things you can do this week** to be a better manager for your team
- **Exclusive discounts** on my services (yep, they're only for folks who have picked up a copy of this book)
- **Ops Playbook Calculator** to learn how much money you're leaving on the table by not implementing the strategies we talked about in the book (get ready for your mind to be blown)
- And more . . .

## Acknowledgments

Thank you to every business owner and team leader who has entrusted me with their story and given me the opportunity to both learn from them and offer support.

Thank you to Caroline Malloy for coaching me through the initial stages of developing this book and your work empowering women nonfiction authors to write the book burning inside of them.

Thank you to my business coaches and mentors who have supported me in my journey into entrepreneurship: Chris Harder, Rebecca Cafiero, Marina Middleton, Jaclyn Johnson, Alli Webb, Adam Schaeuble, Alex Street, Bridgitte Mallinson.

Thank you to Jake Kelfer, Adrienne Dyer, Mary-Theresa Tringale, and the team for helping me bring this book to life.

Thank you to all of my guests on the *Managing Made Simple* podcast who have imparted invaluable wisdom with me and my listeners on making managing easier.

Thank you to my family who cheers me on and offers support every single day and never gets bored of me talking about team operations.

Thank you to my friends who root for my success, amplify my ideas, and keep me laughing along the way.

## Author Bio

Lia Garvin, the "Team Whisperer" provides business owners and team leaders with simple strategies and tools to communicate better with their teams, reduce overwhelm as managers, and turn their employees into profit-generating machines.

She is the bestselling author of *Unstuck,* TEDx speaker, host of the top podcast *Managing Made Simple,* and team operations consultant and coach with experience leading team operations within Google, Microsoft, Apple, and Bank of America.

She is a sought-after expert in the media, featured across Inc, FastCompany, ABC News, CNN Business, US News & World Report, Harvard Business Review, Yahoo, and TV News.

Made in the USA
Middletown, DE
15 February 2024

49145170R00077